STRENGTH FROM WITHIN

ebook ISBN: 979-8-9858895-0-5
Paperback ISBN: 979-8-9858895-1-2
Hardcover ISBN: 979-8-9858895-2-9

Strength from Within

By Amrom Gottesman

CHAPTER 1

By His Parents, at Home

REB LEIBISH WAS BORN in Veča (a small town in Czechoslovakia) on May 5, 1928, to his parents, Reb Avraham Eliezer and Sarah Gottesman, who had been childless for seven long, angst-ridden years. His father would frequently relate how, after so much heartache and yearning, they were *zoche* to a miracle brought about as a result of the *tefillos* of the holy Satmar Rebbe, Rabbi Yoel *zy'a*. Then a second son—Reb Kalman *z'l*—was born a year later. He was the only brother to survive World War II. Yosef, Menachem, and sisters Reichel, Chaya Devora, and Chava tragically perished in the Nazi inferno.

There was no cheder in Veča. However, a little bridge connected Veča to the adjacent village of Šaľa, which boasted a Talmid Torah and even a *Rav*. Conversely, Veča had a *shochet*, Leibish's father Reb Avraham Eliezer, which Šaľa did not. Hence, the two neighboring villages met each other's needs.

Every morning found little Leibish trudging in rain or shine to cheder, alone and unescorted, across the rickety bridge where the local anti-Semitic village lads would lie in wait for the vulnerable young boy and pelt him with stones and taunts. Often, for good measure, they would grab and soil his yarmulke as well. But Leibish was not to be deterred. After all, the motto that he had imbibed from his parents was that the *zechus* of learning Torah was worth suffering for.

Many years later, a woman in Boro Park by the name of Freida Miller *a'h,* who hailed from the village of Šaľa, related that she often saw little Leibish walking home from cheder. When she saw him fearfully hold back as he reached the bridge where the mean-spirited lads were waiting for him, she would take him by the hand and accompany him across the bridge to protect him from his tormentors. She would humorously add, "See what a *talmid chacham* he turned out to be! Imagine if he had not held my hand. He would have surely grown into an even bigger *talmid chacham!*"

The law in Slovakia, as well as in other European countries at that time, mandated that all children attend public school. The teacher in the small village school where Leibish was a student was a vile anti-Semite who delighted in tormenting her Jewish students. One of her favorite torture methods was making a child extend his hand, palm up with fingers joined together, then sadistically rapping his fingertips with a wooden ruler.

One Shabbos morning found Reb Avraham Eliezer walking home from shul, little Leibish in tow, when the malicious teacher sauntered toward them. Reb Avraham Eliezer instinctively greeted her with "*gut Shabbos*" before noticing who she was. Leibish automatically followed his father's lead and likewise said, "*gut Shabbos.*" Only too late did Leibish realize that the woman was in fact the loathsome anti-Semitic teacher who would likely be highly offended at what she would certainly perceive as a deliberate slight.

Sure enough, come Monday, Leibish's premonition was painfully borne out. No sooner had the hapless boy entered the schoolhouse than the teacher viciously pounced on him, slapping him mercilessly across the face as she chanted mockingly, "*gut Shabbos, gut Shabbos, gut Shabbos.*"

In Yeshiva in Pressburg

Eventually, Reb Avraham Eliezer realized that Veča had nothing to offer as far as a Torah *chinuch* was concerned, and in 1936 he sent his two eldest sons, eight-year-old Leibish and seven-year-old Kalman, to the distant city of Pressburg to learn. This required much *mesiras nefesh* and courage both from the parents and the children, who had to fend for themselves in a strange city. This included renting out a room to sleep in for the night, then making their way to the local cheder in the morning, which, of course, had no lunchroom or dining room and no provisions whatsoever. The two youngsters joined the many *talmidei ha'yeshiva* in the prevalent custom colloquially known as *esen teg* by which they received a meal at a different predetermined house of a local resident every day. For every Yom Tov and occasionally for a Shabbos, the two brave boys would travel home to their parents by train—no small feat for such vulnerable young lads.

Like in other cities at the time, secular education was compulsory in Pressburg, and there was a choice of Hungarian, Slovakian, or German curriculum. Because of the vile anti-Semitism he had experienced in Veča, Reb Avraham Eliezer had a distinct antipathy to anything Hungarian and chose to enroll his sons in the Slovakian school. When the Slovakian school did not accept Kalman due to space limitations, he ended up in the German school. This was clear *hashgacha pratis* since his fluency in the German language was later a lifesaver during WWII.

On September 30, 1938, Hungary signed the Munich Agreement with Nazi Germany and Fascist Italy, in which they committed to siding with the Nazis in the event of war. In exchange, Germany facilitated Hungary's retrieval of large swaths of Slovakia that had been seized during World War I—like Galanta, which included Veča and Šaľa and reverted to Hungarian sovereignty.

Shortly thereafter Hungary closed off the newly established borders, blocking off entry and exit to the environs. Leibish, not wishing to be stranded, caught the next train home, much to the relief of his parents. Kalman, on the other hand, caused his parents much angst and worry as he took a bit longer to get his act together and barely made the very last train out of Pressburg, arriving home at 1:00 a.m.

Notably, Reb Avraham Eliezer had succeeded in obtaining from the Slovakian government papers for himself and his family that would have enabled all of them to immigrate to the United States. However, his fear of having to compromise on his children's *chinuch* is what prevented him from actually seizing this opportunity. When the Hungarian government came into power, these papers were rendered worthless.

BRATISLAVA/PRESSBURG GALANTA NITRA

Talmid of Serdahel Rav *zt'l*

The change of regime from Slovakia to Hungary did not bode well for the Jews. It soon became clear that this pact with Germany was no mere territorial transfer. Also incorporated in the pact was Hungarian compliance with the infamous Nuremberg Laws. And indeed, the Hungarians did not lag far behind their German counterparts in their implementation of the vile anti-Semitic decrees—including confiscation of Jewish-owned businesses and properties as well as crushing restrictions and closures of yeshivas.

Eventually, there were only three yeshivas in Hungary that were allowed to remain open: Szombathely, Galanta, and Serdahel Reb Avraham Eliezer very much wanted his eldest son, Leibish, to learn in the renowned Serdahel yeshiva, headed by Harav *Hatzadik* Reb Asher Anshel Katz *zt'l*. It also featured a yeshiva *ketana*, which Reb Avraham Eliezer thought would be especially suitable for his eleven-year-old Leibish.

And so the young stalwart Leibish once again squared his shoulders and departed from his parents' house in pursuit of *limud HaTorah*. Arriving in Serdahel, he started off learning in the yeshiva *ketana* there. However, before long the Serdahel Rav realized that Leibish's diligence and learning skills were way above his age, and he promptly transferred him to the large yeshiva where he learned together with older boys who were serious *lamdanim*. By the time he was Bar Mitzvah, Leibish had an especially warm relationship with the Serdahel Rav and had achieved a reputation as quite a *talmid chacham*.

For Leibish's Bar Mitzvah, his father prepared the customary Bar Mitzvah *pshet'l* for him. However, Leibish felt miffed by the briefness and simplicity of it—something that he later compensated for when he prepared complex, lengthy *pshetlech* for his own Bar Mitzvah boys.

Decades later, here in America, Reb Leibish always recalled the esteem and affection he was accorded by his illustrious Rebbe in his youth and maintained a very close relationship with the Rebbe's son, Harav Yehoshua *zt'l,* Rav of Sombotheli in Williamsburg, and subsequently his sons: Harav Chaim Leib Katz *shlita*; Serdahel Rav, and Harav Asher Anshel Katz *shlita*; Viener Rav.

RIGHT TO LEFT TOP: AVRAHAM ELIEZER, YOSSI, LEIBISH,
KALMAN, SARAH HOLDING CHAYA DEVORA
BOTTOM: MENACHEM, REICHEL

LEIBISH (SIITING IN CHAIR), KALMAN, YOSSI

CHAPTER 2

Ghetto

Nazi Invasion of Hungary

IN THE WINTER OF 1944, black clouds of doom gathered on the Hungarian horizon with the incursion of the Nazis and their constant stream of vicious anti-Semitic edicts. When Leibish was fifteen years old, his beloved yeshiva in Serdahel was closed, and Leibish made his way back home to Veča.

With the ever-increasing decrees and restrictions against the Jews, the Gottesmans felt exceedingly isolated and vulnerable in Veča since there were very few other Jews living there. So Reb Avraham Eliezer moved his family to neighboring Šaľa—a primitive village where there were no plumbing, sewage, or sanitation services. Each family drew their own water from a well, chopped their own firewood for heating and cooking, and dispensed of their waste by interring it in huge dugouts prepared especially for this purpose. Still, the presence of about 120 other Jewish families in the village provided the Gottesmans with a measure of comfort, and they hoped that together they would successfully weather the ominous storm of anti-Semitic persecution until the war would come to an end.

Before long Hungary began confining Jews to ghettos. In March 1944 a ghetto the size of four blocks was established in Šaľa, and no Jew was allowed to set foot outside its parameters. Additionally, a 10:00 p.m. curfew was imposed after which no Jew could be outside then. Less than three weeks later, by April 5, three days before Pesach, there was a new decree issued: every Jew was obligated to wear a yellow star so that they could be easily identified as Jews. The reason for this was blatantly obvious they were now fair game for beatings, taunts, insults, and so on by thugs and ruffians without any intervention from police.

Reb Avraham Eliezer Is Taken Away to Munka Tabor

As is well known, the barbaric Germans had some very loyal assistants in the local Hungarian gendarmes as well as Slovakian brutes, members of the Hlinka Guard, who were only too eager to facilitate the murderous Nazi agenda. It was they who faithfully executed the Nazi injunction to snatch able-bodied Jewish men and dispatch them to forced labor camps. And so, a few days after Pesach, Reb Avraham Eliezer was caught and hurled into a wagon to be taken to what was known as Munka Tabor for military duty.

AVROM LEZER

Kalman happened to be out of the house, tending to some household chores (i.e., fetching firewood, etc.) when his father was seized. Upon his return home, inquiring as to his father's whereabouts, his mother, Sarah, tried to reassure him that "father merely left because of a *shechita* job, which he was called about in a nearby village...oh, and he might have to spend several days there."

But something in his mother's demeanor, something in her tone—perhaps it was the catch in her voice—was unsettling. Kalman knew intuitively that his father had not just left on a voluntary trip...and he was determined to find out more.

Kalman and Leibish, close brothers that they were, had many things in common. Nevertheless, there were some very striking differences between them, both in appearance and in temperament. Just as different were the ways they reacted to and dealt with the endless trials and tribulations they faced over the course of their tragic experiences.

Leibish was tall and slender, thoughtful, and even-keeled. Conversely, Kalman was short and portly, impulsive, and energetic. Without any thought about the prohibition against Jews venturing out of the ghetto, Kalman leaped onto his bicycle and pedaled furiously toward the train station, yanking off his yellow star as an afterthought. He arrived at the station just in time to see Hungarian gendarmes steering a large group of Jews onto a waiting train. Kalman's heart sank as he noticed a familiar figure. There was his father being roughly shoved forward onto the train. As the train pulled out of the station, Kalman stood frozen in grief, his heart telling him that he would never see his father again.

Kalman returned home despondent and, in a choked voice, related what he had just seen. As the children all sobbed brokenheartedly, their mother stoically put aside her own grief and comforted the dejected children. "We have a *groise bashefer*, and He will watch over Tatty just like He watches over all of us." Likewise, when distraught neighbors and friends came to the pious Sarah to unburden themselves, weeping for their bereavement and loss, she consoled and comforted them with encouraging words of *chizuk* and *bitachon*.

At first the family received some correspondence from Reb Avraham Eliezer. In one letter Reb Avraham Eliezer wrote that there were three other Jewish men in the camp with him. And as a *shochet*, he was also able to procure some kosher poultry for himself and the other Jews. All in all, the anxious family received a total of three letters from Reb Avraham Eliezer. Then there was nothing. The family continued to hope and pray, but it turned out that Reb

Avraham Eliezer ended up in the infamous Mauthausen death camp where he perished.

'Sarah *Imeinu*' Prepared to Sacrifice Her Children on the *Akeida*
Right after Pesach 1944, the German savages, aided and abetted by the loyal Hungarian gendarmes, rounded up all the Jews of Šaľa and issued the following proclamation: All Jews will be transferred to a local brick factory. Everyone may take along their personal belongings not to exceed the weight of fifty kilos.

Sarah Gottesman was not shocked by this development. She had known all along that it was only a matter of time before they would all be rounded up. She had a brother, Mendel Schlesinger, who had lived in Vienna and had fled to Switzerland in 1938 at the beginning of the Anschluss. Since then Sarah had made a point of drilling into her children's minds the name and address of their uncle in Switzerland. "Who knows what will be? If the situation in Hungary becomes really bad, perhaps you can try and reach him."

מענדל שלעזינגער אן בערטע

MENDEL AND BERTA SCHLESINGER

Now, after the Germans announced the imminent removal of the Jews, Sarah had a flash of inspiration. Very circumspectly, she removed her rings and slipped them into Kalman's hand, whispering, "I know that you are very resourceful and will, *IY'H*, survive and return here. Go hide these rings somewhere so that you will find them upon your return."

Kalman obediently trudged outside and made his way to the huge pits behind the house that were used to dispose of waste, hoping to conceal the rings there. But to his chagrin, the area was crawling with eagle-eyed soldiers who insisted that he must not linger there since they had to leave immediately. Kalman felt momentarily lost. How could he fulfill his mother's instructions? Suddenly, he had an idea. Turning to the soldiers, he bowed his head and respectfully asked that they allow him two minutes privacy for "bathroom use" near the dugout. After warning him that he better make it fast, they left him alone there for a couple of minutes, and Kalman deftly concealed the rings there.

All too soon, the dismal group of Jews were led through the village streets to the train station. Along the way, Sarah Gottesman recognized the gypsy woman who had been her domestic helper for many years, assisting her with laundry, cleaning, and so on. This was very common throughout many areas of eastern Europe at the time. There were many homeless, vagabond gypsies roaming the countryside, many of whom very much welcomed the opportunity to perform domestic chores for a very low wage.

This particular gypsy woman had been in the Gottesman household for so long that she knew quite a bit of Yiddish and almost considered herself part of the family. Now, when she saw the family being led off into the unknown, she ran after her former employer, yelling, "*Shochet neni* [a nickname by which Sarah Gottesman was frequently called], wait! You have such beautiful daughters. It's a real shame to have them murdered in cold blood, which they will likely be. Why not leave them with me? I will raise them as my own." Sarah turned to the gypsy woman and replied firmly, "No, thanks. The Creator of the world gave me these children. And I will hold onto them for as long as He lets me. If He so wills it, I am prepared to return them to Him."

Confined in the Brick Factory

The Jews from Šaľa were loaded onto the train and transported to a nearby brick factory, where they were detained for several weeks. The brick factory consisted of a vast, open area with minimal protection against the elements. The only food they had to eat was the little that they brought from home. Every day more and more groups of Jews were unceremoniously dumped there. Eventually, there were more than six thousand wretched people—men, women, and children—languishing there under miserable conditions that simply defy description. There were no toilet facilities, and there was no water to be had. There was, of course, nowhere to lie down except on the cold ground. Ruthless German soldiers strutted around, snapping their batons and brandishing their rifles. Small children cried piteously while mothers were helpless to do anything. Pandemonium and chaos reigned supreme.

Sarah Gottesman and her seven young children were somewhat "fortunate" since they arrived on the earliest transport. Hence, she was able to secure a "better" spot. She also managed to obtain some broken bricks that she piled up around her as a pathetic shelter of sorts, which gave them some illusory privacy, albeit no protection from the elements.

There were several *Gedolei Yisrael* who likewise "sojourned" in that wretched brick factory courtyard (i.e., the Šaľa Rav, *Harav Mordche Strasser zt'l*; the elderly ninety-two-year-old Lakomayia Rav *zt'l*; and the renowned Galanter Rav, Harav Yehoshua Buxbaum, *zt'l; HY'D*). These *tzadikim,* as all other *rabbanim* they came across, were viciously singled out for especially brutal treatment. Reb Leibish would recall with anguish until his dying day how the venerated Galanter Rav was slapped viciously and resoundingly across the face before and after having his beard forcefully shorn off.

It was said that serious rescue efforts were underway on behalf of the Galanter Rav, facilitated by the well-known wine magnate, Reb Yonah Herzog, who had business dealings with the Germans. However, the Galanter Rav categorically refused to abandon his *kehilla*, opting instead to remain with them until the bitter end.

CHAPTER 3

Auschwitz

Destination Auschwitz

THE HAPLESS JEWS WERE kept within the confines of the brick factory for almost two months. Throughout this time, the German beasts—as was their wont—tried to delude their captives into believing that no evil would befall them and they needed to remain calm. The plan was merely to dispatch able-bodied people to work for the Third Reich, so they would have all their needs met.

Finally, the unfortunate Jews were "liberated" from the brick factory. And what kind of liberation it was! All the Jews who had spent the last two desolate months in the open courtyard of the brick factory yard were unceremoniously loaded onto windowless cattle cars (no toilet and no seats, except for the floor) and taken to their final destination: Birkenau, Auschwitz.

Tragically, most people had no concept of the significance of Auschwitz and believed that it would be an improvement over their current dismal conditions where the ongoing chaos and incessant crying and whining of so many miserable children reverberated in their ears twenty-four hours a day.

This trip to the ultimate hell was itself a living Gehinnom. People stood tightly pressed against each other for three days and three nights while the weeping, restless children were placed on the floor. Their piteous cries for food and water pierced the air. There was one pail in the corner of each wagon to be used as a toilet. People trying to reach the pail, in the darkness of course, inevitably ended up stepping on the children, who could only whimper feebly by that time.

The train stopped in several cities, such as Budapest and others, before reaching the final destination. Some fellow travelers took notice of the two teenage boys, Leibish and Kalman, and urged them to leap off the train at any of the stops, rather than continue on to Auschwitz. However, Leibish did not have the temerity and guts to do that. Kalman would have been inclined to consider it, but by then his mother was quite sick and very weak, and he did not want to leave her.

The Nazi guards, who, of course, knew very well where the train was headed and were very much aware of the fate that awaited the doomed passengers, went around demanding all jewelry and valuables—as if that would somehow make a difference in the conditions that awaited them. The poor Jews had to leave all the belongings they carried with them in the train, after which the Jews were immediately taken to the crematoriums.

On June 11, 1944, 20 Sivan, the train arrived at Auschwitz. However, perhaps because it was Sunday and the "overworked" Nazi fiends needed their day of "rest," or whatever the reason may have been, the wretched human cargo was made to remain in the squalid, reeking cattle cars all day.

After nightfall the metal doors clanked open, and Nazi guards began viciously herding the weary passengers off the train, announcing repeatedly that they could not carry any of their belongings with them. They could only take the clothes they were wearing. So Sarah Gottesman, like so many other hapless mothers, instructed her children to put on as many layers of clothing as they could. Additionally, she surreptitiously stuffed the pockets with some cans of sardines and other paltry edibles that she could salvage from her pathetic baggage.

As soon as the Jews stepped off the train, they were struck by the sight and smell of billowing smoke coming out of the gas chambers. Of course, they could not imagine what it was. In fact, decades later when recalling those horrific events, Reb Leibish said that in the few initial moments of their arrival at Auschwitz, he naively thought the smoke was emanating from the chimney of a bakery. Tragically, he found out all too soon what those black plumes of smoke were about.

Before long, the weary Jews were lined up like so many sheep for *selektzia* in front of the Malach Hamoves incarnate, Dr. Mengele, *ym'sh*. With a delicate flick of his white-gloved wrist, he sent millions of people to the left side, to their immediate deaths. Or, if they were deemed fit to work, to the right, for a life worse than death, in the forced labor and concentration camps where they were starved, beaten, tortured, and worked to death.

Typically, strong, healthy-looking youths from eighteen years and older were sent to the right since they could be expected to perform productive work for the Third Reich, while young children and older, weaker people were sent to the left to join those slated to be immediately, cold-bloodedly murdered in the gas chambers. Leibish, who was tall for his age and was wearing several layers of clothing, which added to his body mass, was sent to the right, while Sarah and her six younger children were sent to the left.

Suddenly, one of the Polish men who was performing forced labor there, guarding the Jews, keeping them in line until they entered the gas chambers, and subsequently sorting through the mountains of personal belongings of the victims, stopped in front of Kalman and his younger brother Yossi. "Quick!"

he whispered to them. "Go to that side! And when they ask you how old you are and what is your occupation, say that you are eighteen years old and that you are an experienced field worker." When the boys hesitated, not wanting to leave their mother, the man yanked them both out of the line they were standing in and propelled them to the other side. "Believe me. I know what's going on here. I've been working here for five years already." And in a flash, this man, who had clearly risked his life to save theirs, was gone.

While the Jews were huddling at the gate of Auschwitz, most did not realize the full horror of the fate that awaited them; and the Nazi beasts deliberately tried to mislead them into thinking that nothing terrible would befall them. After all, it would be much easier for the murderers to exterminate unsuspecting, passive victims. There was a camp nearby, fenced in by electric barbed wire, where the newly arrived Jews could see haggard-looking women staggering around in striped uniforms. The Nazi guards noticed the frightened glances of the newcomers and hastened to "explain." "See those women there? They really have it good. Even at night when they're already wearing pajamas, they frolic around!"

However, the deception was quickly dispelled. As soon as the long-suffering, starving inmates noticed the newcomers, they began piteously clamoring for a piece of bread or anything else they might have to share. The newcomers were so overwhelmed with horrified pity that they reached into their own ragged pockets to share the last scraps of food they might have still had. As the sympathetic newcomers tossed the paltry morsels of food over the fence to the starving inmates, a burly German guard suddenly appeared, rifle cocked. "Whoever will throw anything over the fence will be immediately shot!"

And so Leibish, Kalman, and Yossi stood helplessly as their beloved mother and younger siblings were carted away. Although the young boys may not have known it at the time, it was only a matter of hours, on 26 Sivan, June 17, 1944, until their mother and her young innocent children joined the millions of other precious Yidden whose lives were brutally snuffed out in the gas chambers of the Third Reich.

A MEMORIAL PLAQUE STONE IN ISRAEL FOR THE JEWS OF ŠAĽA AND THE SURROUNDING
SUBURBS, INCLUDING VEČA, WHO PERISHED IN AUSCHWITZ OR MUNKA-TABOR.

The Brothers Are Separated

Those "lucky" Jews who were sent to the right, including the three brothers
Leibish, Kalman, and Yossi, were first taken for delousing and showers. All
their clothing was confiscated; they were allowed to keep only their belts and
shoes. Some Jews resourcefully managed to conceal some items within their
belts and shoes.

The next phase of treatment was a "sterilization" process, which consisted of having all hair shorn off—including body hair (e.g., under the arms, etc.)—using a razor blade that was extremely painful as it inevitably sheared away pieces of skin as well. Many of these unwilling "barbers" were Jewish men who were forced to perform this sadistic task on their own brethren.

While the freshly shorn men were smarting from the cuts and gashes all over their bodies, they were washed down with benzine and turpentine and scrubbed with hard bristle brushes. This was followed by a shower that deluged them with scalding hot water, which was then followed by a stream of ice-cold water, intensifying the pain of the tormented Jews. Finally, they were given the infamous striped uniforms, making them official Auschwitz inmates.

The new inmates were once again lined up, and a Nazi officer again asked each of them what their occupation was. Of course, no one had any documents there to prove or disprove any assertions. So, recalling the mysterious Polish man's emphatic advice, Kalman and Yossi both claimed *land verchaft* (field/farm work). They responded similarly to the question of their age. Both duly purported to be older than they were. Consequently, they were sent to Birkenau, a subcamp of Auschwitz, which served as a "holding lager" from where they were eventually dispatched to various concentration camps across Poland and Germany to engage in brutal forced labor, starvation, and unimaginable torture.

Conversely, those who naively admitted to being younger than the German barbarians deemed "age appropriate" were detained in Auschwitz for a brief stint of inhumane, torturous forced labor before being summarily dispatched to the gas chamber to join the millions of *kedoshim* who had preceded them, as well as the many, many more who were still to follow them.

The inmates of all the concentration camps were made to perform inhumane, backbreaking work to benefit the German war effort. That was the only reason they were allowed to live, not that there was any effort to keep them alive. On the contrary, the wretched inmates had only the striped uniforms to wear in icy cold weather and the guards starved, beat, and physically and mentally tormented the prisoners like only Nazi sadists can. Disease was rampant, and people died like flies. However, that was not much of a problem for the lager commandants, since there were plenty of replacements to be had. All the manpower any concentration camp needed was easily available in Birkenau, where there were plenty of doomed Jews who were allowed to live for the exclusive purpose of serving the glorious Third Reich.

At this point, Leibish was separated from Kalman and Yossi who, being younger, were kept in Auschwitz. Leibish was sent to Birkenau to await transport to whichever concentration camp the Nazis saw fit. He spent four torturous, brutal weeks there in the bitter cold, with no place to sleep and hardly any food, since he was not assigned to any specific work detail there.

There was a very precise and consistent food distribution system in place. Everyone there received a quarter of a loaf of bread every day. Those inmates who were assigned to a labor detail were the "lucky" recipients of another quarter of a loaf. Technically, a person might be able to subsist on half a loaf of bread a day; however, a quarter of a loaf was woefully inadequate to sustain a person all day, and starvation and hunger pangs were a consistent presence.

As mentioned, Leibish and his fellow inmates were made to sleep on the cold earthen floor of an empty barrack without any blanket or covering. Due to lack of space, the Nazis set them up in increments of five, sleeping in a sitting position between each other's legs. When one of them needed to get up to relieve themselves, it created havoc within this distressed human pyramid. With only one bathroom in the whole barrack, the devastations of morning relieve are indescribable in words. Leibish retrieved then a cold which developed to pneumonia.

In addition to their physical travails, the hapless prisoners were repeatedly taunted by the barbarous Nazis who delighted in pointing to the columns of smoke emanating from the crematoriums, which they gleefully explained were from the burning corpses of their murdered parents and siblings. This information left the anguished inmates devastated and shattered beyond comprehension.

The Auschwitz prison population also included the indigent, nomadic gypsies who roamed the European countryside in tribes. Like the Jews, the gypsies were considered undesirables in the German vision of a Third Reich with a "pure" Aryan race. Hence, both the Jews and the gypsies needed to be exterminated.

The gypsies were aware that some Jewish prisoners had managed to conceal some "valuables" in their shoes and/or within their belts. So they would circulate among the Jewish prisoners in Birkenau and try to cajole them into giving up some of those valuables, sometimes in return for a promise of some scraps of food. Then, abruptly, one day there was no sign of the gypsies anywhere in the camp. Strangely, they had all been suddenly and inexplicably eliminated. Such was the unpredictability of life/death in Birkenau.

After four long weeks, Leibish was finally placed on a transport to a German concentration camp.

CHAPTER 4

Kindness in the Night

Kalman and Yossi Recite *Parshas Ha'Mon*

KALMAN WAS FOURTEEN YEARS old when he arrived at Auschwitz, while Yossi had just turned thirteen. Leibish did not see his two younger brothers after their separation. However, after the war was over and he was liberated, Leibish was reunited with his brother Kalman, who filled him in on some of the incredible suffering he and Yossi had sustained.

Kalman and Yossi were hurled into a barrack, where they were kept without a morsel of food or drop of water. After four torturous days, the two brothers were almost delirious from starvation. In their innocence the two young brothers, filled with *emuna* and bitachon, hit on a "plan." Kalman, the elder one, spoke softly to his famished younger brother. He recalled learning in cheder and subsequently in yeshiva that reciting Parshas Ha'mon was a *segula* for sustenance (e.g., bread, etc.). Somehow, at that point, Kalman still had his siddur, and the two boys managed to daven every day and to don tefillin. Now, the two starving brothers began fervently reciting Parshas Ha'mon, certain that food would soon be forthcoming. But, alas, the minutes and hours ticked by, and their stomachs continued to growl painfully. And much to their consternation, nothing resembling food appeared.

"Perhaps we didn't say it with proper *kavanah*," Kalman suggested to his young, ravenous brother. "Let's try again." And so they did. Slowly and

21

painstakingly, with their last ounce of strength, the two brothers again recited Parshas Ha'mon, and once again there was no miraculous appearance of food.

"Maybe the problem is that you don't understand the meaning of the words," Kalman rationalized. And with that he proceeded to interpret the words into Yiddish while Yossi listened intently and nodded along weakly. When Kalman finished his recital, the two starving boys turned their eyes heavenward and waited expectantly. Still nothing.

For a long time both boys lay listlessly on the bare wooden planks, wondering why the *segula* wasn't working. Finally, Kalman sat up and said to Yossi, "You know, today is Friday. Let's prepare for Shabbos. We'll daven *kabbolas Shabbos*, then we'll eat a *seudas Shabbos*. We'll sing *zemiras*, just like we did at home.

As night fell, they pretended to go to shul and daven, then come "home" from shul, sing *Shalom Aleichem*, make *kiddush*, and sit down to a *seuda*, replete with *zemiros* and *divrei Torah*. Finally, the two emaciated boys, wracked by the most debilitating hunger imaginable, fell into a fitful sleep. On Shabbos morning they were jolted out of their sleep by the sonorous voice of a German officer. Although they were momentarily terrified, it turned out to be the answer to their fervent prayers.

"Who speaks German here?" the officer demanded. Almost all hands shot up. After all, they all spoke Yiddish, which did somewhat resemble German. Clearly a divine *shaliach,* the officer selected four men, including Kalman Gottesman. "How do you know German?" the officer demanded.

"I attended the gymnasium in Bratislava; they taught German there," Kalman replied meekly.

Until his dying day, Kalman could not fathom why, from the entire barrack, the German officer chose him. "Come with me. I have an important job for you," he beckoned to Kalman. With some trepidation Kalman followed the officer, who led him to the so-called hospital and showed him into a room. "This room is your responsibility," he instructed Kalman. "You are to make sure that it is clean and tidy at all times."

In truth, this was a hospital in name only, and nary a patient was ever cured there. In fact, all the sick and infirm people that were brought there were summarily shot and killed. The hospital was intended as a front to show the Red

Cross how well the inmates were being tended to. But for Kalman this was truly a Godsend. The officer led him to a storage closet where clothes were kept, told Kalman to choose something suitable, and even gave him a badge to wear on his arm, which would ensure him free access to the facilities.

The clothing was, of course, very welcome, but much more important was the food that came along with the job. Apparently, reciting Parshas Ha'mon was indeed quite a *segula*! It turned out to be more effective than he could have hoped for.

From that point, Kalman was the "lucky" recipient of a half of a loaf of bread—officially double the amount that other inmates were getting. Additionally, there was a substantial amount of food delivered to the hospital every day, ostensibly for the patients. However, since the patients were instantly eliminated upon their arrival, there was an abundance of food that was simply disposed of. Kalman, taking advantage of his badge and the "prestige" that came with it, surreptitiously made his rounds to the trash bins and collected the discarded food, which he discreetly passed on to Yossi. Finally, they were seeing the miraculous results of the tried-and-true *segula* of reciting Parshas Ham'on!

When the other famished inmates realized that Kalman had access to precious food and was so generously sharing it, they all surrounded him and desperately clamored for some morsels to assuage their perpetually gnawing hunger.

Sadly, before long, the Schutzstaffel (SS) supervisor took note of Kalman's "illegal" distribution and called him out for it. After giving him a stern warning about his "criminal" activities, he handed Kalman a whip. "Here," he said. "If those filthy wretches approach you again and ask for food that's not coming to them, use this whip freely to disperse them. That'll teach them!" It goes without saying that Kalman never even considered carrying out these instructions and would never, in any way, hurt a fellow Yid. Still, much to his chagrin, he was now in the very painful position of having to decline his brethren's heartrending pleas for a morsel of food when he had access to plenty. But he clearly had no choice and tearfully apologized to the ravenous Jews as he implored them to back off or risk getting them all into serious trouble.

One day Kalman was approached by a desperate Yid whom he had known as a respectable, well-to-do man back home in Slovakia. "Kalman," the man begged. "Perhaps you can find a job for me too in the hospital you are working in. I'm desperate for some food." Kalman looked at this formerly rich man. "Look," he told him. "I really don't know of any suitable job for you. But I do know that the hospital could really use someone to clean the latrines." The desperate man didn't hesitate for a second. "I'd love to have the job. I can't take this hunger any longer." And so it came about that this once proud, wealthy man was "fortunate" enough to land a job cleaning latrines, which undoubtedly helped him survive the war.

Kalman Leaves Auschwitz; Yossi Departs This World

Because Kalman started working in the hospital, he no longer slept in the same barrack as Yossi. It just so happened that Yossi's barrack was the unfortunate recipient of numerous visits from Dr. Josef Mengele. The purpose of these frequent visits was to examine the inmates for scarlet fever, which was rampant there. Of course, all those suffering from this devastating disease were systematically dispatched to the gas chambers via the notorious *selektzias* that Mengele nonchalantly presided over.

Kalman was always an energetic and resourceful lad. Although he was barely fourteen years old, he was a devoted father figure to his younger brother, who was much more helpless and vulnerable. Kalman repeatedly urged Yossi to "man up," keep his wits about him, and try to avoid danger. Any time the wicked Mengele showed up to conduct a selection, for example, Yossi was to make himself scarce and hide out in the latrines until the peril had passed. Furthermore, Yossi was to be extremely careful (as if that were possible) to avoid contracting scarlet fever. Kalman also worried that Yossi was looking very gaunt and not eating enough. So he told Yossi to wait for him every night near the second post of the barbed wire fence and Kalman would, risking his own life, pass him some extra food from the hospital.

Sadly, however, all Kalman's heroic efforts could not protect his young brother from this deadly and highly contagious disease. And eventually, the emaciated Yossi succumbed to scarlet fever and ended up standing in the dreaded *selektzia* line. Kalman had somehow, *bechasdei Hashem,* found some favor in the eyes of the SS officer at the hospital, and he beseeched him to pluck his brother out of the selektzia line. Incredibly, the officer did, and Yossi was allowed to return to his barrack. But the brothers' relief was short-lived because Yossi once again found himself in the selektzia line during Mengele's next ill-fated visit. With a trembling heart, Kalman again approached the "friendly" SS officer and begged him to intervene, which he did, albeit not quite as readily as the first time.

As Kalman watched Yossi shuffle listlessly back to his barrack, Kalman's heart contracted. He had a feeling that it was only a matter of time before Yossi would again fall prey to Mengele's ruthless selektzias. He knew he couldn't count on his SS "friend's" repeated intervention. If Yossi ended up in Mengele's clutches once again, Kalman would voluntarily join his younger brother in the selektzia line, naively hopeful that he would somehow manage to extricate both of them.

Evidently, the Nazis were maliciously familiar with the Jewish calendar and used this knowledge to execute their cruel agenda. They scheduled their sadistic deportations and selektzias to coincide with *yamim tovim*. On Yom Kippur, Yossi's barrack was once again "honored" with a visit from the Angel of Death, who had come to conduct another one of his deadly selektzias. When Kalman heard about this, he rushed over and slipped in among the columns of doomed prisoners, certain that he would be able to slip out with Yossi before they were hauled off to the gas chambers—but not before he asked someone to relay a message to the SS officer who helped him in the past.

Sure enough, the officer arrived and sought out Kalman from among the horde of hopeless, defeated shells of human beings. However, much to Kalman's chagrin, the "kindly" officer was apparently done with his rescue efforts. Clearly he was not going to bail Yossi out—or even Kalman for that matter. Instead, he offered to bring Kalman a loaf of bread, which Kalman categorically declined because it was Yom Kippur. The SS officer then informed Kalman that he could not do anything more for him today…maybe tomorrow. Kalman understood all too well what this meant. They were all going to be taken to the gas chambers today. By tomorrow they would all be gone.

Kalman's mind was working feverishly. He was not going to stand by meekly and wait to be taken to the gas chambers. Looking out the window, he noted the throngs of people milling about, mostly relatives of those doomed individuals who had fallen prey to the selektzia. They were desperately hoping for some last-minute reprieve whereby they could whisk their loved one out of that ill-fated line. Others hoped to at least have the opportunity to bid their soon-to-be murdered relative farewell. Kalman also noticed piles of cartons and boxes lying around, and suddenly, he had a flash of inspiration. Very surreptitiously, he approached four other men in the line and shared his plan with them. "Look here," he said to them. "As matters stand now, we are all doomed to die in the gas chambers. Look outside," he said, pointing to the chaos outside the barrack. "I suggest that we all dash outside simultaneously, each of us in a different direction, blending into the crowd and hiding among the boxes. Hopefully, we will all elude the Nazis. Or even if, *chas vesholom*, one of us is pursued and gets caught, the rest of us will still stand a chance."

And so it was; Kalman managed to elude Mengele's henchmen and made his way back to the hospital where he immediately sought out the SS officer who had helped him in the past and tearfully begged him to once again intercede on his brother's behalf. The officer, who was surely surprised to see that Kalman had managed to escape the selektzia, informed him curtly that after three attempts to save his brother, he could not do it again. Kalman then approached another SS officer with whom he had struck up an acquaintance and implored him to save his brother from the selektzia. Surprisingly, the officer agreed, made his way over to the barrack, and yanked Yossi out of the line.

Later, the "friendly" SS officer at the hospital pulled Kalman aside for an honest conversation. "Listen," he told Kalman. "You must realize that all your frantic efforts to save your brother are for naught. Eventually, everyone here in Auschwitz will be eliminated. The only ticket to survival is to be transferred to Germany to a labor camp to do some useful work for the Third Reich war effort." He paused before adding, "However, both you and your brother are too young to be sent to a German labor camp. So you might as well save your efforts."

When Kalman heard these words, he realized that he had to face reality. If he stayed in Auschwitz with Yossi, they were both doomed to end up in the gas chambers. If he would somehow manage to escape Auschwitz, there was a possibility that one of them would survive. One of the inmates in Yossi's barrack appeared to be, like Kalman, a spirited, plucky go-getter. Kalman approached him and charged him with the responsibility of looking out for Yossi to the best of his ability. As a token of appreciation, Kalman gave him a sizable amount of food that he had salvaged from the hospital.

Finally, Kalman went to take his leave from Yossi. He told him that he felt he had to leave for Germany and had arranged for a competent, strong man to watch out for him. He also told him bluntly that one or both of them might not live to see the end of the war. "If you are fortunate to survive the war, remember what Mother told us: We have an uncle, Mendel Schlesinger, in Switzerland, and you ought to try to find him."

Kalman set out for the train station and waited for a train that was headed to Germany. When the train arrived, mobs of people tried to push and jostle their way onto it. Conscious of his very young age, Kalman wisely avoided the front and the rear of the line, so as to be as inconspicuous as possible, and managed to shoulder his way in somewhere in the middle of the line of people desperately streaming onto the train.

In the meantime, Yossi continued to languish in Auschwitz until Simchas Torah came around and Mengele, *ym'sh* once again, true to form, appeared to conduct his disastrous selektzia. And like the last time, Yossi once again ended up in the ill-fated line destined for the gas chambers; only this time around, there was no one there to even attempt any rescue efforts on his behalf. On Isru Chag Succos, 24 Tishrei, Yossi, like so many millions of his brethren, was cold-bloodedly murdered in the gas chambers.

As the wretched hordes of Jews were herded into the gas chamber, their Nazi captors wickedly decided to have some fun. "The first fifty people who can run really fast will be allowed to escape," an SS officer announced gleefully. Later, it was one of these escapees who confirmed to Kalman that his brother Yossi remained in the gas chamber, sharing the fate of his mother, siblings, and millions of his Jewish brethren.

CHAPTER 5

Dachau

Allach

ON JULY 11, EXACTLY one month after his arrival to Auschwitz, Leibish arrived at Allach, part of the infamous Dachau concentration camp, which included dozens of subcamps within a fifty-mile radius. Allach was the main transfer center right near the central train station where people arrived from Auschwitz and were then transferred to the various subcamps in Dachau. Leibish spent two weeks in Allach before being transferred to Mühldorf, a subcamp of Dachau where prisoners were made to perform all kinds of forced labor under the most barbaric conditions imaginable.

Most of this camp's labor assignments revolved around the heavily fortified underground Waltz factory that produced the notorious Messerschmitt bomber planes. This factory was built in a way that was meant to withstand any attempts of attack or sabotage by the Allied forces. To that end, the emaciated Jewish inmates were forced to erect the requisite eight-foot-thick concrete walls.

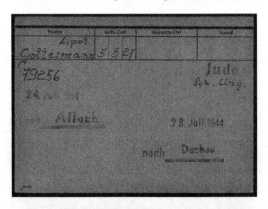

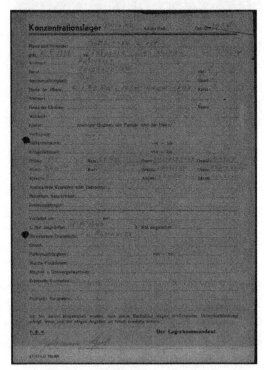

DOCUMENTS CREATED BY THE SS IN ALECH

The Miseries of Mühldorf

Mühldorf was comprised of two separate camps. While neither of them was quite a vacation resort, the "Waldlager" (so called because of its location deep inside the forest) was known as one of the most brutal concentration camps that included backbreaking labor and notoriously brutal conditions. There were underground barracks where the exhausted slave laborers slept for a few paltry hours every night.

It was in this lager that Leibish was interned, as were many prominent rabbanim like Harav Ahron Teitlebaum, the Nirbater Rav *zt'l*; Harav Yidel'e Gottlieb *zt'l*, Rav of Mishkoltz; Hagaon, Rebbi Yitzchok Zev Meir *zt'l* subsequently Nitra Rosh Yeshiva.

As mentioned, the work at Mühldorf was excruciating. The weak, starving Jews were forced to excavate mountains and haul away the heavy loads of rocks and soil, which were ground up and made into cement that was then carted away by other inmates.

There was a well-thought-out system in place whereby the Jews were divided into groups with a different *kapo* presiding over each group. The work site was dotted with little booths where the *kapos* were stationed, from where they supervised the slave laborers, making sure they weren't slacking off. Every dawn and dusk found the weary inmates lined up in front of those booths for the infamous *Appell*, or roll call.

Only after the Appell added up and each and every prisoner was accounted for did the exhausted, starving inmates receive their meager scraps of food. However, if there was any discrepancy (i.e., the count was one number off), panic ensued. Everyone had to remain standing ramrod straight while the guards set off with search dogs to find the unlucky culprit. If it turned out that the prisoner had, as so often happened, simply expired from all the torment and anguish, then the very inadequate food distribution could continue. But if the missing inmate was discovered alive, his transgression was dealt with by one of two methods: he was villainously beaten to within an inch of his life, or he was summarily shot.

Unfortunately, a discrepancy during Appell was an all-too-common scenario, and Leibish and his comrades in misery got to be the reluctant observers of many sadistic beatings and ruthless killings. In one instance, the hapless fellow was pummeled and punched in the stomach until he fainted from the pain. He was then revived, after which the pummeling resumed. When he once again lost consciousness, the Nazi brute revived him once again. This tragic scene was repeated several times until the bruised and beaten man finally returned his soul to his maker.

The Mishkoltzer Rav was singled out for particularly brutal treatment, perhaps because the vile Germans realized he was a *rabbiner*. Many years later his grandson, a fine *talmid chacham*, married Leibish's granddaughter.

On the Wrong Truck

In Mühldorf, Leibish had to trek a distance of about sixty to ninety minutes every day to fetch the cumbersome sacks of cement, then lug them back to the underground factory. Starved and debilitated, Leibish had no strength to make the long trek, let alone carry the heavy sacks back to the factory. And because he was tall, the standard striped lager uniforms were short and skimpy on him, leaving much of his body exposed to the bitter cold. Additionally, time was of essence, and he couldn't walk at a slow pace since he had to rush to be back in time for the Appell.

Very often, Leibish's sole nourishment consisted of potato peels. Notwithstanding his severe starvation and malnourishment, Leibish had to clamber up steep mountainous terrain and hoist huge, heavy cement sacks back to the barracks. The load was so ungainly and cumbersome that Leibish frequently folded beneath its weight. However, there was no time to wallow in self-pity. Before he even had a chance to catch his breath, he had to pick himself up and resume his trek or risk the wrath of the Nazi brutes.

After two weeks of this unimaginable torture, Leibish collapsed and fell to the ground unconscious. He was taken to the so-called clinic in the camp, where he was diagnosed with acute pneumonia and a very high temperature. The clinic staff at Mühldorf decided to send Leibish to a "better" clinic in the main Dachau lager for treatment, ostensibly because they were better equipped to deal with the more serious cases. However, the real reason for the transfer was much more sinister: the glorious Third Reich had no use for Jews who were ill and unproductive, nor did they consider it worthwhile to heal them. After all, there were plenty of Jews available for forced slave labor. Dachau had several gas chambers precisely for this purpose. Jews from the surrounding camps who were too ill or too weak to work were sent there for quick and expedient extermination. Also, adding to the convenience was the availability of several mass graves into which the murdered Jews could easily be dumped. And last but not least, there were various medical experiments conducted there on the ailing Jews, similar to what the fiend Josef Mengele performed.

It is worth recalling the words of the Belzer Rav, Rav Ahron, *zy'a*. Every Jew who survived that horrific epoch surely had to have had a *malach elokim* at his side. What transpired with Leibish is living proof of that concept.

There were a number of prisoners of war (POWs) of various nationalities interned along with the Jews in some concentration camps. Notably, they were treated very differently from the Jewish inmates, since they were protected by international laws regarding the treatment of POWs. Jews, of course, had no such protection. Hashem orchestrated matters so that Leibish was inadvertently placed on a truck with POWs who were actually being transported to a real clinic in Dachau with real doctors and real medical treatment, as opposed to the gas chambers. This was a real miracle, and what followed was mind-boggling.

NOTE LEIBISH BROUGHT ALONG FILES FROM MÜHLDORF

An Angel in Human Form

The attending doctor in the clinic, Dr. Drust Yehn, who was of Dutch origin, examined Leibish and immediately realized that a mistake must have been made. This patient was clearly no POW. He was way too sick and malnourished for that. So how did he end up here? In a barely audible voice, Leibish related to the doctor that he was a Jew, an inmate in the Mühldorf concentration camp. The doctor was visibly moved by Leibish's pathetic state. "Don't worry," he reassured him quietly. "Everything will be okay. I will do all I can to help you." Then, incredibly, the doctor took Leibish's ID card, which had the letter *J* stamped on it, indicating that he was a Jude, and deftly changed the *J* to an *S* for Slovak. (This wasn't such an untruth since Leibish did indeed hail from Slovakia.) This meant Leibish could remain in the clinic and receive whatever medical treatment the doctor was able administer.

Leibish was gravely ill and literally on the verge of death, drifting in and out of consciousness. While unconscious he had repeated visions of his mother sitting by his bedside, reciting *Tehillim*. Dr. Drust Yehn took Leibish under his wing and dedicated himself to Leibish's care with incredible devotion until he, *Baruch Hashem*, recovered.

After the war ended, Leibish felt obliged to seek out the good doctor and thank him for saving his life while risking his own. After much effort, which included poring over Dutch telephone directories, Leibish managed to track down Dr. Drust Yehn at his house. When the doctor himself answered the door, Leibish's excitement knew no bounds. In a tear-choked voice, Leibish said he came to thank the doctor for all that he had done. But to his utter shock, the doctor looked at Leibish blankly. He had no idea what Leibish was talking about and even denied having been in Dachau!

Leibish did not know what to make of it. Perhaps the doctor realized that his neighbors were not especially fond of Jews and was therefore loath to even discuss that he had saved the life of a Jew. But Leibish was more inclined to believe that his savior was none other than the *Malach Refoel* in human form.

Although Leibish recovered from his bout with pneumonia in Dachau, there was some residual scarring of the lungs, which remained a concern throughout his life. After one particularly dire pronouncement by a pulmonologist many years later, Leibish spoke anxiously to his Rebbe, Harav Michoel Ber

Weissmandl. What would be with his young children if he were to take ill? Rav Weissmandl reassured him that he needn't worry; Hashem would surely take care of His children if something, *chas v'shalom*, happened to him. Remarkably, however, Leibish never experienced any flare-up in his lungs and never had any breathing issues, even though severe scarring was consistently present in all future chest x-rays. This was just another link in the chain of miracles that Leibish experienced.

Mesiras Nefesh for Torah and *Mitzvoth*

After Leibish miraculously recuperated, he remained in the main Dachau concentration camp, which was divided into blocks. Each block contained about thirty barracks. Leibish was placed in block thirty, which was designated for those inmates who were sickly and infirm with compromised abilities to perform rigorous labor. Accordingly, they were given only scraps and leftovers. When all the soup had been doled out, for instance, the empty pot was filled up with water and reboiled. This "soup" was then given to the inmates of Block 30.

The hunger and starvation that Leibish suffered during those winter months is unimaginable. Additionally, with almost no shoes or clothing, he suffered bitterly from the intense cold while performing grueling labor outside. The barracks where the men slept were not heated, nor were they insulated against the frigid cold. They slept on hard wooden bunks and were given straw-filled sacks that were to serve as both mattresses and covers.

Due to the filthy, unsanitary conditions, everyone there was infested with body lice and suffered from a whole host of diseases (e.g., cholera, typhus, diarrhea, and others). These were as debilitating as they were contagious and reduced the victims into *Muselmänner*—wan skeletons, barely resembling human beings. These pathetic shells of humans were usually promptly eliminated by the Nazis—sometimes by shooting and sometimes by being dispatched to the gas chamber.

Leibish, like so many others there, had reached the stage of Muselmann. And once again, a *malach* from heaven intervened to keep him alive. Leibish experienced *nissim* on two fronts: first, that he survived the dreadful illness, and second, that he was not dispatched to the gas chamber.

The exhausted, bedraggled, and freezing men were expected to rise at 4:00 a.m. in preparation for the Appell. Some of the barracks had latrines adjacent to them, while other latrines were a considerable distance from the barracks.

Each and every inmate was obligated to be outside for the Appell by 6:00 a.m., regardless of the temperature or the weather. Through rain, snow, hail, and below-freezing temperatures, the miserable prisoners, wearing nothing but threadbare rags, had to stand ramrod straight for the Appell, which usually lasted about thirty minutes. And woe to the hapless individual who arrived late or didn't stand up straight enough. All too often, the punishment for this transgression was death.

Hunger, cold, and illness notwithstanding, the frail sixteen-year-old lad had to abide by the brutal work schedule set forth by the Nazi beasts. Once when he was standing barefoot outside in subzero temperatures—wearing nothing but tatters—the soles of his feet literally froze to the cold concrete floor. That was the proverbial straw that broke the camel's back, and Leibish burst into tears. However, he quickly pulled himself together and plodded on, drawing strength from his emuna and bitachon. His determination to be *mekayem* whatever *mitzvohs* he could bolstered his morale and enabled him to go on, despite all the suffering and peril he faced every day.

As a *talmid* in Pressburg and in the Serdahel Yeshiva, Leibish learned how to prepare a Hebrew *luach* (calendar). This knowledge served him well in the concentration camp when, using the secular calendar, he was able to determine when it was Rosh Chodesh and Yamim Tovim.

Leibish tried to be scrupulous not only with Shmiras Shabbos but also with Motzei Shabbos. To that end, he would carefully put away a morsel of bread so that he could wash for Melava Malka when he would also sing *zemiros*.

On the night of Purim 1945, Leibish returned to his barrack after a long, freezing, grueling day at work. As weak and exhausted as he was, sleep eluded him. He was haunted by poignant memories of Purims past. Only last year he had celebrated Purim with his friends by the Serdahel Rav. In his mind's eye he relived the ecstasy, the inspiration, and the *simcha* that permeated the atmosphere; and now...no *megillah*, no Purim *seuda*, only hard wooden slats in a freezing cold barrack.

Dispiritedly, he eventually fell asleep and experienced a most delightful and uplifting dream in which he was sitting at a Purim *tish* together with the Serdehal Rav and the Galante Rav. Everyone was merry, eating and drinking in a true spirit of Purim. Leibish awoke, suffused with *chizuk* and strength to persevere and do whatever it took to survive this Gehinnom.

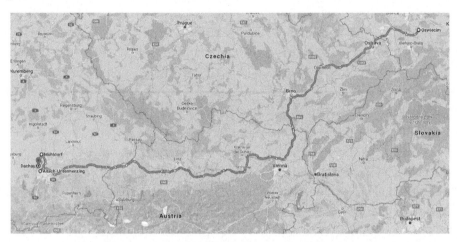

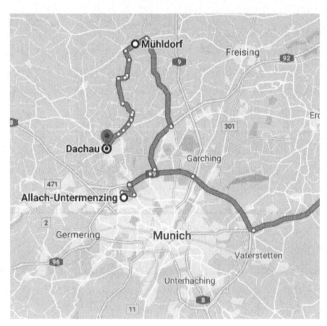

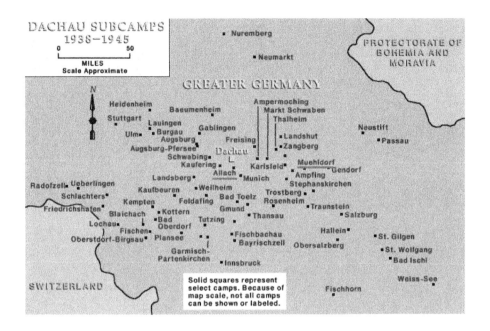

CHAPTER 6
Ray of Light

Yaakov Springer

EVEN IN THE DARKEST and bleakest of circumstances, Hashem sent Leibish a ray of light to dispel the abject gloom. In Dachau this ray of light came in the form of a man, Yaakov Springer.

YAAKOV SPRINGER

Until his dying day, Leibish spoke about Mr. Springer, as Leibish called him. Although at age fifty he was much older than the sixteen-year-old Leibish, the two developed a very close bond and consistently looked out for each other. This most likely kept them both alive and enabled them to survive the harrowing tortures of Dachau.

Mr. Springer settled in Germany after WWI, where he got married and raised his children. Whatever the level of his religious observance might have been there, when he was in the concentration camp, his Jewish spark certainly shone and sparkled. He had sterling *middos*, a heart of gold, and was always prepared to help out another Jew.

At that time, in 1945, he was already fifty years old—probably the oldest inmate in the concentration camp. As is tragically well known, the German fiends kept alive only "productive," young, and healthy people who were able to work for the Third Reich. Hence, a fifty-year-old man was very much a rarity there. The trials and travails of the Springer family began in 1938, following Kristallnacht. So when Leibish met Mr. Springer in 1945, he had already suffered through seven years of Hitler's Gehinnom—one year in Germany and six more years in various concentration camps.

Right at the onset, when the dark clouds of doom began gathering over the horizon, Mr. Springer tried to send his two sons away so that they might avoid the tragic fate of their brethren. However, in the course of his internment in different concentration camps, he lost contact with his sons and with his wife. Predictably, he was very anxious as to their whereabouts, and his hopelessness and depression intensified with each passing day.

One day he noticed a sickly, young lad who was all skin and bones. Remarkably though, as broken as this young boy was in body, that's how hale and wholesome he was in spirit. Many of the weary, starving inmates had, over time, lost every vestige of dignity and self-respect. Every waking minute was spent either doing grueling, backbreaking labor or engaged in a primitive, animalistic obsession with food. There was no trace of morals or manners. Sadly, driven by unbearable hunger and desperation, one didn't hesitate before pouncing on someone else's portion of food when the opportunity presented itself, and arguments and fights were commonplace.

But Leibish was different, Mr. Springer noted. Leibish radiated an inner peace, a serenity that comes from the firm, unshakeable knowledge that Hashem is in charge and everything that happens is according to His plan. And all his actions, his behavior and manner of speech, reflected that. Leibish was clearly connected to Hashem and tried to observe whatever *mitzvohs* he could in those bitter conditions.

Mr. Springer was immediately taken with the young lad who displayed such poise and dignity in such harrowing circumstances. He struck up a conversation with him, and before long, the two became close friends. Leibish told Mr. Springer about his parents and siblings and how much he missed them, and Mr. Springer told Leibish about his wife and two children whom he missed dreadfully. Neither of them knew whether their families were still alive, and both sobbed uncontrollably in their mutual anguish. After a while, the older man pulled himself together and tried to comfort his newfound young friend, encouraging him to remain hopeful and not give up. Leibish felt buoyed by Mr. Springer's empathetic compassion and, drawing on his own boundless emuna and bitachon, offered the older man *chizuk* by sharing with him the story of Iyov that he had learned in Yeshiva. Mr. Springer listened raptly as Leibish recounted how Iyov had suffered so many unspeakable calamities before he merited blessed salvation.

"You and I are also afflicted, like Iyov was, by trials and tribulations beyond the human scope," Leibish said to Mr. Springer. "And just like Hashem helped Iyov, he will surely help us too."

Leibish and Mr. Springer were assigned to different work details, but every evening they met in the barracks. Mr. Springer was consistently amazed by Leibish's dignified faith and vast knowledge as well as his strength of character. He watched as Leibish never lost his equilibrium and always avoided arguments and fights.

The more Mr. Springer observed Leibish, the more impressed he was with him, and he was determined to help him in whatever way possible. Eventually, he began bringing Leibish crusts of bread, which he saved from his own meager portion. When Leibish categorically refused to accept them, Mr. Springer would place the crusts near Leibish and simply walk away. Finally, Leibish took those crusts and saved them for Melave Malka.

For the remaining months of their incarceration, the steadfast bond between Leibish and Mr. Springer is what helped them both survive the terrible Nazi Gehinnom.

Interestingly, although Mr. Springer was older and had many more painful years of experience in suffering, it was sixteen-year-old Leibish with his deep-seated emuna and unswerving Torah connection that helped Mr. Springer through many trials and tribulations.

Hashem Sends Food in the Wilderness

Mr. Springer was a proficient shoemaker, a skill he picked up in the concentration camp and one that served him very well there as a "business opportunity," so to speak. People would bring him their shoes to be repaired or ask him to make them a pair of new shoes. They compensated him with the best, most desirable currency in Dachau—food. Obviously, Mr. Springer could not devote much time to his "business" since he had his tasks that he needed to perform for the Nazis. However, after he finished the requisite work for the German war effort, he would toil over a pair of old shoes or fashion a new pair of shoes, thus earning a few morsels of food, which often spelled the difference between death by starvation and life.

One day a fellow inmate of Belgian origin approached Mr. Springer and requested that he make him a pair of shoes, for which he would pay him with Belgian pastries, which, even in the best of times, were famed to be the best in the world. This was indeed an unimaginable treasure!

Incredibly (but predictably), no sooner had Mr. Springer received the coveted pastries than he sought out Leibish and gave him some. Leibish (predictably) was unwilling to take this hard-earned delicacy out of the mouth of the older man. But Mr. Springer firmly insisted, and Leibish guiltily accepted the very generous gift—one that he recalled with gratitude for the rest of his life, pointing out to his children and grandchildren how the selflessness of this man literally saved his life. He would add with a smile, "See, even in Dachau, if Hashem wanted to, He would send someone not just plain food, but Belgian pastries!"

Over time Mr. Springer's shoe-making talents were very much in demand, with more and more people clamoring for his services. Leibish realized that the extra food Mr. Springer was earning from his shoe-making business was put to very good use. Namely, the kindhearted Mr. Springer was on the lookout for Jews who were on the verge of starvation and selflessly shared his precious, hard-earned food with them. Leibish came up with a brilliant plan; he would step in to complete Mr. Springer's obligatory tasks for the German slave drivers, in addition to his own workload, thus enabling Mr. Springer to work at his shoe-making business full time and earn the priceless food that he shared so generously with Leibish and with the other starving inmates.

And so it was. Over the next few weeks, Leibish performed a double quota of work—his own and Mr. Springer's—while Mr. Springer plied his shoe-making trade, earning enough food to sustain Leibish as well. Theirs was the epitome of mutual devotion in a reciprocally beneficial relationship.

Two Kinds of Bombs

In March 1945 an ominous rumble could be heard more and more frequently. However, to the ears of the Jewish captives in Dachau, it was the sweetest sound they could hope for. It meant that bombs were being dropped by the Allied Forces on the not-too-distant city of Munich. Eventually, the hopes and prayers of the long-suffering prisoners were realized, and the bombs started falling ever closer to Dachau. Almost daily the alarm would go off and the SS officers would scatter and flee to the shelters.

One day a bomb landed with a loud thud right in the center of the camp. Astoundingly, though, it did not explode and wreak havoc and destruction. This was a "chocolate bomb"—a huge parcel of assorted foods and goodies given by the Red Cross and intended for the starving camp inmates. Not surprisingly though, the SS officers intercepted the "delivery," ensuring its disappearance before any Jewish inmate could enjoy even one morsel of it.

The following day the roar of an airplane flying overhead was followed by leaflets fluttering down from heaven. Although the Nazis tried their utmost to prevent the inmates from accessing them, rumors soon began spreading like wildfire. The leaflets were printed in several languages and urged the inmates to remain strong and persevere since liberation was imminent.

As the explosive booms of bombs detonating came ever closer to the Dachau camp, the "chocolate" bombs landing in the center of the camp became more frequent. By now, the SS officers were sharing some of the goodies with the non-Jewish inmates but still made very sure that the Jewish inmates got none of it.

However, indirectly, the victuals did eventually make their way to the hungry Jews via Mr. Springer. He received more requests for shoe repairs from non-Jews who now had the wherewithal to pay for them.

Mr. Springer's Breakdown

At that time something terrible happened to Mr. Springer. He got up one morning and seemed to have totally lost his bearings. Apparently, six years of the inhumane suffering that he endured took their toll. He seemed to be in the grip of some type of psychotic episode that prevented him from eating, sleeping, and/or communicating with people. He would roam around the barracks aimlessly, not talking to anyone. He lay on his bunk, eyes wide open but unseeing. All attempts by Leibish and others to engage him and draw him out were futile.

Leibish tried desperately to protect Mr. Springer as best as he could. Besides going to work and completing Mr. Springer's tasks as well, Leibish spent every waking hour at the sick man's side, soothing him, caressing him, and reassuring him that he wouldn't leave his side until Mr. Springer was well.

Since Mr. Springer wasn't touching his food anyway, Leibish took it and offered it to one inmate who was a doctor by profession, begging him to try to help Mr. Springer. The doctor came over to Mr. Springer's bunk and proceeded to examine him, poking, prodding, and massaging until, after a while, Mr. Springer wordlessly indicated that he was thirsty. This was the first time he had communicated anything to anyone since the onset of his episode.

While this was indeed very encouraging, the problem was that there was nothing available to drink in Dachau. Eight ounces of tepid tea were distributed to the prisoners every day—that was it. Without any hesitation, Leibish made the magnanimous decision to give his own tea to Mr. Springer. This went on for the next two weeks as Mr. Springer slowly regained his strength and his bearings.

After two weeks, Mr. Springer suddenly burst into sobs that lasted hours on end. It was as if the spigot of his emotions had sprung open and all the pent-up pain and anguish of six years was pouring forth. Finally, emotionally spent, his gaze fell on Leibish as if he was seeing him for the first time. All these days and nights when Leibish kept vigil over Mr. Springer, giving him his own ration of tea and so much more, seemed to have gone unnoticed!

Slowly but surely, Mr. Springer recovered. His eyes became more focused, and he recognized people and engaged with them. In sharing his experience with Leibish, he told him that in the past few weeks, for the duration of his illness, his vision—his perception of his surroundings—was hazy and blurred, much like a near-sighted person who had his spectacles removed. Now, he explained, he felt like his eyeglasses had been returned to him. Still, he remained very weak with hardly any appetite for the meager crust of bread they received.

Leibish and other inmates joyfully told Mr. Springer about the advances of the American military and how they were decimating German cities. Surely, the end of their suffering was near. There were even whispered rumors about liquidating the camp! However, in his weakened state, Mr. Springer did not even comprehend the magnitude of these developments.

Mr. Springer wanted desperately to live to see the end of the war so that he might be reunited with his wife and children. Just thinking about them infused him with life and strength. Slowly, he began performing small jobs again, sewing up a pair of crude stockings for one, fashioning a pair of shoes for another. As mentioned, working for the non-Jewish inmates was a very lucrative enterprise now that they were the recipients of generous Red Cross packages and could pay well for his services. These goodies actually kept him alive, since bread was woefully inadequate, and the so-called soup that was doled out to the inmates was disgustingly rancid and not fit for consumption.

This time when Mr. Springer wanted to resume his habit of sharing some choice morsels with Leibish, the latter adamantly refused to eat them. Instead, he took the food and hid it until later when he fed it to Mr. Springer at an opportune time. Mr. Springer eventually became more engaged with his surroundings and displayed an animated interest in the latest war news.

Eventually, news filtered in that the Russian and American forces had already reached well into German territory. Needless to say, all the prisoners were jubilant, but for Mr. Springer in particular, this news was the best medicine he could have gotten. Suddenly, it seemed like his hopeful dreams of freedom and reuniting with his family might soon be realized. Once again, Leibish and Mr. Springer, the two loyal friends, encouraged each other to remain strong and optimistic, telling each other that their salvation was surely imminent.

Chaos in Dachau

Despite the mounting rumors about the imminent evacuation of Dachau, the reverse happened. As the bombardments intensified, the Germans began moving inmates further away from the front, and there was a sudden large influx of inmates into Dachau, apparently the last Nazi holdout. It got to the point where the camp became terribly crowded, with inmates being bedded down in the narrow space between the blocks. An additional two thousand inmates were crammed in.

Due to the chaos created by the surge of new inmates, most of the work assignments were suspended. These newcomers brought along a host of contagious diseases that quickly spread throughout Dachau, and people fell like flies. On their way to the latrines, inmates would literally have to step over dead bodies that littered the ground. Some of them had been shot by the Nazis, while others simply succumbed to illness and starvation.

The situation was extremely dire. The camp was unable to provide food—not even at the paltry level they had been providing up to that point. Because the roads were bombed and destroyed, it was impossible to bring in food from outside the camp. Also, inexplicably, the longed-for food parcels from the Red Cross that had been such life savers for the starving Jews ceased to fall from the sky. The daily bread rations dwindled from one bread per person to one bread per ten people. Malnourishment and starvation worsened beyond anything imaginable today.

At this point, without the distraction of work, the emaciated Jews just lay lethargically on their hard wooden bunks or roamed aimlessly around the camp. For diversion, and to take their minds off their gnawing hunger and suffocating conditions, they resorted to picking the nits off of and killing the lice on their ravaged, unwashed bodies. There was nothing else they could occupy themselves with. After all the months of harrowing torture and suffering, it was during this period—as they were wallowing in filth, ravaged by disease, and overcome by hunger, thirst, and boredom—that it seemed to the Jews they had reached rock bottom. Would they ever lead normal, happy lives again?

One day the inmates were summoned to the designated place of assembly for an important announcement: all inmates were to be transferred to Allach—the original arrival point in the Dachau concentration camp complex, where the train station was situated. Ostensibly, the reason for the move was the availability of "hospital blocks" there where the sick and infirm could be "treated."

Knowing what they knew by now about the Germans' modus operandi, the Jews foresaw what awaited them in Allach, and it did not bode well for them.

An SS doctor examined the haggard, half-dead inmates and duly documented his diagnoses and recommendations as to who needed to be hospitalized. Mr. Springer's name was included on that ill-fated list, generating much dismay among his camp mates, who knew that this was a one-way trip to the gas chamber. There was no evasion or circumvention that anyone could think of. But when Hashem decrees life, He has His ways of facilitating it. In this case, Mr. Springer's and many other Jews' deliverance came in the form of the simple nonappearance of the transport train that was supposed to take them to Allach and certain death.

In the meantime, American planes could be seen flying over the skies of Dachau. The SS officers attempted to shoot them down to no avail. The inmates craned their necks to follow the planes' trajectory and were bewildered and disappointed that not a single bomb onto SS facilities landed in the camp. And incredibly, more and more transports of prisoners kept arriving, further depleting the already meager resources of food and space. What was going on? What was taking so long? When would they be liberated? What nefarious plans did the Nazis have for them now?

The suspense and uncertainty were unbearable. Leibish and Mr. Springer devised their own coping mechanism. Mr. Springer simply took a virtual trip back to a different world in a previous life that included his wife and children and all the pleasures and gratifications he had known there. And suddenly, he was happy. His spirits soared, and he beamed as he regaled Leibish with his delightful fantasies that so pleasantly replaced the bitter reality.

Leibish, in turn, offered his friend words of emuna and bitachon that he had imbibed from his parents. So between the two them, they had both *gashmius* and *ruchniyus*. Mr. Springer constantly marveled at the strength of spirit of this young lad who retained such warm memories of his parents' teachings. It also gave him a glimpse into the superior, uplifting existence of religious Jews.

A Roller Coaster of Hope

By the end of March, it seemed as if the transport to Allach to the "hospital barracks" would finally take place. A doctor once again examined the prisoners to determine who (supposedly) required hospitalization. At this point, both Leibish and Mr. Springer felt that it would be a good idea to leave Dachau at all costs. Surely, conditions elsewhere couldn't be any worse. The Nazis could not possibly exterminate an entire transport of Jews with the American forces so close by.

Leibish was prepared to join the transport headed to Allach, while Mr. Springer was fearful of doing so because his name appeared on the list of sick people who he suspected would all be gassed. He decided to try to avoid the transport to Allach and blend into the crowds of prisoners who were eagerly waiting to be liberated by the Allied Forces. Still, he urged Leibish not to remain in Dachau and to attempt to join the transport to Allach. But by now Leibish was so attached to Mr. Springer that he would not consider leaving without him.

At 6:00 p.m. on April 1, the prisoners were once again ordered to assemble in the square where they had gathered daily for the Appell. The expectation was that the transport would now finally take place. They were made to stand there for endless hours into the night. Adding to the torture and discomfort was the onset of a freezing downpour of rain, snow, and hail, which left the bedraggled, emaciated prisoners drenched and freezing to the bone.

Finally, past midnight, the exhausted inmates were ordered back to the barracks. But for some unknown reason, when they got to the barracks, they were not allowed inside and were made to remain outside throughout the dismal rainy night, with no place to lie down or even sit. The most they could do was huddle against the cold concrete wall and doze fitfully while standing up. Still, with all the chaos in the camp, the Nazi brutes persisted in their fiendish routine of waking their hapless prisoners at 4:00 a.m. and sending them to the washrooms to wash up.

After the excruciating ordeal of the previous night, many of the prisoners did not have the strength to make the trip to the washrooms and just collapsed on the cold concrete floor. Leibish and Mr. Springer felt very disheartened as they counted no less than thirty dead bodies sprawled on the ground on their trek to the washrooms. Eventually, Mr. Springer reassured both himself and Leibish with the rationale that if they were being sent to the washrooms, it had to mean that the Nazis' intention was not to kill them. Hopefully, liberation really was imminent.

In the washrooms, the inmates were disinfected prior to being given a set of flimsy, ill-fitting "clothes" that did nothing to keep the cold (or the lice) at bay. At 8:30 a.m., the exhausted inmates were ordered yet again to assemble in the Appell place, where they were left to stand under the open sky, unprotected from the elements, for two entire days.

After so many emotional ups and downs, with hope being raised and then quickly dashed, the anguished Jews realized that the Nazi fiends could not be taken at their word. All their talk of transport which then never materialized, followed by talk of another nonexistent transport, taught the Jews that the German brutes were just out to torment them in any way possible. Finally, word filtered down from the main office that there would not be any transport out of Dachau, and everyone was to return to their barrack.

This roller coaster of raised hopes that were so cruelly dashed was very draining. Upon their return to the barracks, the broken shards of human beings were depleted both physically and emotionally, and they became walking shadows. The food rations were slashed even more, with one loaf of bread allocated to more than ten people. And, based on precedent, the starving prisoners expected their rations to be further reduced with each passing day.

There were some rumors circulating about a prisoner exchange that the Germans had clinched with the Americans whereby wounded German POWs would be freed in exchange for Jewish concentration camp inmates who would be sent to neutral Switzerland. Many inmates grasped at these rumors, desperately wanting to believe them. But it quickly became clear that these rumors were just that—baseless, unfounded rumors with no connection to reality.

Out of One Gehinnom, into Another

Mr. Springer was arguably the most seasoned, experienced concentration camp inmate in Dachau. Realizing that, at least for now, they were remaining in Dachau, he tapped into his innate resilience and determined to make the best of it. Falling back on his old trade, he began sewing and patching the flimsy clothes of the prisoners and repairing their broken, worn-out shoes. Like before, the payment currency was food or any other edibles, which he generously shared with Leibish and others.

The most miserable torture during those final two weeks was the plague of rumors. Every day there were fresh rumors being circulated: the camp is being liquidated, inmates are being relocated to a different camp, inmates are being freed, and so on. A different story, a different report every day—many of them deliberately started by bored inmates who created their own version of events in their fertile imagination, then shared their fantasies and illusions with others.

But the SS beasts did not take very kindly to these rumors. Even as they were on the threshold of defeat, they designated kapos to quash these rumors. The cruelty of the kapos as they wielded their sticks and batons exceeded that of the Nazis. But to the half-dead remnants of human beings who had all but given up on life, the vicious beatings made hardly a dent in their psyche. Engaging in fantasy and reverie was the only way out of their anguish and torment as chaos and hunger intensified every day.

Leibish and Mr. Springer were now back in their original block and were pretty much isolated from the other inmates, except for those who sought Mr. Springer's services. They didn't get to hear any war news and had no idea what was going on at the front. Still, the hint of imminent liberation was in the air. Some indications of that were, firstly, the fact that there was no more forced labor going on, and secondly, that the roar of bomber planes overhead no longer pierced the air, which could only mean that the Allied Forces were already on the ground close by. "It won't be long now; you'll see," Mr. Springer and Leibish told each other soothingly. "Maybe we'll get to Munich, which is under American control now," Mr. Springer ventured hopefully.

The old rumors about Jews being transported to Switzerland resurfaced when a Bavarian doctor arrived at the camp to examine the inmates and determine who was capable of walking any distance unaided. Unsurprisingly, most inmates were so frail they could hardly stand, let alone walk.

"Looks like you'll need to join the transport," the doctor concluded. These words led many to believe that perhaps there was something to the rumors about transports to Switzerland after all. Still, there were niggling, uneasy doubts in the hearts of many. Yes, there was finally going to be a transport, but who was to know where the transport would take them? Would it be to Switzerland, to "hospitals," which meant gas chambers?

After several agonizing days of doubts and uncertainty, there was an announcement ordering everyone to take their belongings (which, if anything, consisted of some rags) and assemble in the Appell place. As the wretched prisoners dutifully hobbled toward the square, flanked by SS officers with rifles drawn, they were filled with conflicting emotions. Would things finally get better? Or would the SS bomb the entire camp? The latter notion seemed, to some, as feasible as it was chilling. Wouldn't bombing the camp with the thousands of inmates in it be the easiest quickest way for the Germans to rid themselves of what was becoming an increasingly bigger burden to them?

However, Mr. Springer chose not to believe that frightening theory and chastised Leibish for even speculating about it. "Are you really going to accept at face value all the dismal predictions of every pessimistic doomsayer? After all we've been through and survived, are we going to panic now? Let's just take one step at a time and hope for the best."

As it turned out, this time, the much-talked-about transport actually materialized. Later that day, the Germans began herding the Jews to the railroad tracks outside the camp. As they trudged past the barbed wire fence, Mr. Springer paused just long enough to raise his hands heavenward and declare, "Thank you Hashem for allowing me to survive and to leave Dachau alive twice. To those people who speak fearfully of Gehinnom, I want to say that surely Gehinnom can't be any worse than Dachau."

CHAPTER 7

En Route to Mass Elimination

Out of the Concentration Camp, but Not Liberated

AFTER SO MUCH SUSPENSE and angst, waiting for a transport that might or might not arrive, the weary Jews couldn't believe that they were finally standing near the train tracks, hopefully on the verge of a normal, peaceful life. So they stood and waited…and waited…but no train arrived that day. Or the next day, or the day after.

Finally, after two weeks of waiting, the bone-weary, half-dead Jews heard the rumble of a train approaching. When the train finally pulled into the station, the Jews could not believe their eyes. This was unlike any train they had seen in a long time. They were used to being transported by freight trains or cattle cars—the kind that had been used to bring them to Auschwitz and later ship them off to Allach and Mühldorf. This was a decent train, replete with passenger seats and windows, most of which were broken, but still…a train designed for transporting human beings!

After the incessant, dehumanizing torture they had suffered, their self-image was so downtrodden that the Jews couldn't fathom being transported in such upper-class fashion. And where would these "magnificent" trains be taking them? To Switzerland or perhaps another safe place of refuge? The questions swirled fast and furious through their minds. Surely, they weren't being transported to the gas chambers in such magnificent trains.

The shattered Jews were about to allow themselves to believe that maybe, finally, they were going to be treated like normal human beings. But apparently, the cup of their affliction was not yet full. As they were standing and gazing with rapture at this "beautiful" train that they were so eager to board, the locomotive, which propelled the train, was detached and whisked away, taking with it the dreams and hopes of the disappointed Jews.

Several hours later, there was still no sign the locomotive was supposed to return for them. Much to their bewilderment, a row of trucks suddenly appeared. What could this possibly mean? What evil plans did the Nazis have in mind for them this time?

By now Leibish had had enough of rumors and speculations and was determined to get to the bottom of what was going on. Noticing a Hungarian officer, he approached him and struck up a conversation with him. Apparently, at this point, with German defeat in the air, the frosty arrogance so typical of the Germans' lackeys had somewhat dissipated and the officer actually deigned to answer Leibish's queries—especially since Leibish spoke to him in his mother tongue. He informed Leibish that, to the best of his knowledge, the Germans were not planning to exterminate the Jews at this point. Instead, the plan was to transport them by train to a secure place further away from the front. As far as the trucks were concerned, he reassured Leibish there was nothing sinister about them. On the contrary, the trucks were sent by the Red Cross, were filled with food and other necessities, and were accompanied by two Red Cross officers.

When Leibish shared this information with Mr. Springer, the latter was somewhat skeptical. But even as they were talking about it, they noticed two Red Cross officials preparing to distribute parcels of food. Mr. Springer was stunned. "Wow!" he exclaimed excitedly. "Could it be that we left Gehinnom and entered Gan Eden?"

Overcrowded—How Long Will the Plan Last?

On Tuesday, April 24, the order came for everyone to board the train. It turned out that the Nazis were able to take a train designed for humans and render it into one with subhuman conditions. There were twenty people sent onto each car, accompanied by an SS officer. However, each car contained only eight seats with a long, narrow aisle between them as well as two overhead luggage racks on each side.

Since Mr. Springer was the oldest person in the car, and his solicitous care for Leibish had not gone unnoticed, he was unanimously chosen by all twenty passengers and the SS officer of his car to be responsible for maintaining order and avoiding arguments and bickering.

Mr. Springer took his responsibility seriously and rose to the task. Looking around briefly, he immediately came up with a creative solution to the problem of accommodating twenty passengers in an eight-passenger car. The eight seats would have to make do for ten passengers, in other words, five people on four seats. Another five people could stretch out on the overhead luggage racks, and five people could sit or lie on the floor. After a couple of hours, the passengers would trade places. Resultantly, everyone will have a chance to have a decent seat (albeit somewhat squashed), will spend some time stretched out on the overhead rack, and will have a turn standing up or sitting on the ground.

This system seemed to work, and nobody complained. It was certainly an improvement over the barracks in Dachau. And anyway, they hoped it wouldn't be long before they would arrive at their destination. Mr. Springer's age stood him in good stead and earned him respect. The situation in the other cars was very different, with passengers squabbling and bickering incessantly.

After ascertaining that the situation in the car was under control, the SS guard left the train to confer with the SS guards who oversaw other cars. He came back bearing good tidings. The Red Cross food parcels would now be distributed, and he needed a volunteer who would be responsible for the equitable distribution among the twenty passengers of his car. One young passenger stepped up to the plate, and before long everyone was clutching a priceless parcel of sublime food.

Mr. Springer would recall years later, "No one who wasn't there could ever imagine what these parcels meant to us. After months and years of subsisting on dried crusts of bread and putrid, gravelly soup, we were suddenly given normal, tasty food!"

Mr. Springer and Leibish pored over their food parcels together and couldn't stop marveling at their magnificent contents. And like the devoted father figure that he was, Mr. Springer urged Leibish to exercise self-control and refrain from eating too much or too fast because it would adversely affect his health. Tragically, many famished prisoners died as a result of overindulging, which their shrunken digestive systems could not tolerate. Leibish heeded Mr. Springer's advice and exercised restraint, eating only small quantities at a time. As he relished every delicious morsel, he was moved to tears. His self-esteem was suddenly restored. He was worthy of real, normal food that was fit for humans, not just measly scraps fit for farm animals. For the first time in many months, he experienced the feeling of being satiated—the total absence of hunger pangs.

While the food parcels were indeed a delight, much to the frustration of the passengers, the train remained in the station—minus the locomotive. Apparently, the ray of light from the end of the tunnel was still bleak. Liberation was tantalizingly close, but they were still confined; instead of a large concentration camp, they were being held in a small, cramped railcar.

Every railcar had a metal bucket, which was meant to be used by the passengers as a lavatory. However, as mentioned, there was no floor space since every inch was strewn with people. The bucket needed to be held in the lap of a passenger so that another might use it. Predictably, no one was keen on doing that; in fact, no one wanted that bucket near them at all. The bucket, therefore, remained with the individual who used it last. When someone who was lying on the overhead luggage rack needed to use the bucket, they would have to clamber down and tread on other passengers.

The SS officer stood by the door and did not allow anyone to leave the train. In each car there were twenty weak, sickly people cramped together. Some had typhus, others were suffering from dysentery, and still others had other afflictions. Yet no one was allowed to leave the train. Unsurprisingly, the stench was unbearable—even though the glass in the windows was missing and there was some air coming in.

As the day gave way to night and the train still wasn't going anywhere, the miserable prisoners began to panic, feeling that this new Gehinnom was just as bad as the one they were coming from. As the stench worsened, so did their restlessness and intolerance. Arguments and bickering could be heard from every car.

Once again, Mr. Springer stepped up to the plate, soothing and calming volatile tempers. "Come on, Yidden," he pleaded. "Just be patient for a little bit longer. You see that we have, *B'H*, left the camps. Surely, we are on the verge of salvation. If the Nazis planned to kill us, they could have easily done so. They wouldn't have bothered placing us on the train, distributing the Red Cross parcels, and so on. And what's more," he continued, "clearly, this is no picnic for the Nazi guards stationed in every car. They don't enjoy being here with us, stench and all. Let's all calm down. You'll see; we will all soon be free."

No one had a watch, but when Mr. Springer estimated that it was about midnight, he decided that in order to retain some structure and sanity, it was time to have the passengers change places to provide a semblance of equity. But this was no small feat. It was as complicated as a colorful Rubik's Cube. Finally, the following strategy was agreed upon: The five people perched atop the luggage racks were to clamber down, which inevitably meant treading on the five people on the floor. Then the five people sitting on the passenger seats scramble up to the luggage rack while the people on the floor wrestled their way out from underneath the people who were stepping on them, to take their places on the passenger seats. Finally, the second group of five people settled themselves on the floor.

This entire process took quite a while, considering the pathetic conditions of the skeletal Jews who barely had the strength to move, let alone clamber up and/or down. Still, it gave everyone a chance to stretch their muscles, and at the end of the exhausting process, everyone settled down.

Mr. Springer then suggested that everyone try to get some sleep. "Let everyone be quiet and refrain from talking until sunrise. This will give us all a chance to recoup our strength," he urged his car mates. Mr. Springer's words were well received, and for a while, a nocturnal quiet prevailed throughout the car.

Train Not Moving, but Two Jewish Lives Saved

At dawn Mr. Springer noticed that the forty-year-old man sitting across from him appeared extremely weak, so much so that his head was completely lolling to the side. Mr. Springer bent forward and gently tried to straighten the man's posture. But the issue was not the posture; it was simply a general malaise stemming from so many months of torture and starvation, which finally caught up with him.

While bent over him, Mr. Springer heard the man's barely audible whisper, "Thirsty...I'm so thirsty." Mr. Springer tried encouraging the man to wait until morning when he would try to fetch him some water, then suddenly remembered the Red Cross parcel, which this feeble man had surely not even opened. Mr. Springer found the unopened parcel and rummaged through it until he discovered some milk. But when he tried to feed some of it to the sick man, he made the painful discovery that the man was unable to swallow. Without opening his eyes, the man gestured hopelessly that he couldn't swallow and wanted to be left alone.

It was Wednesday, April 25, and the train still stood as if rooted to its spot—no movement whatsoever. However, Mr. Springer had something more pressing on his mind: the poor man, barely alive, with his head slumped to the side. With much difficulty, he edged his way out of the car and approached the guard to ask him for permission to fetch some water from the locomotive. Looking at him disdainfully, the guard replied coldly, "I don't know what locomotive you're talking about. As of now, there is no locomotive here."

Feeling resigned, Mr. Springer returned to the car only to discover that he had more to worry about than that extremely ill man who could not even hold his head up. A young man, apparently suffering from typhoid fever, was so ill that he was unable to sit up altogether. But how and where could he lay down in this terribly overcrowded, cramped car?

Miraculously, Mr. Springer managed to access some boards, which were then suspended across the width of the car and thrust underneath the two people lying on the overhead luggage racks. Then the typhoid patient was placed atop that board.

Later in the morning, the guard came aboard the car and made a very welcome announcement: there was water to be had in a nearby structure, and he would allow some men to go together with Mr. Springer to bring water for all those stranded on the train. This was indeed very welcome news and gave everyone's spirits a much-needed boost. It also gave them a bit more space, at least for the time that it took the men to return with the water.

Upon his return, Mr. Springer made the stunning declaration that, miracle of miracles, the water was hot! He then proceeded to take some instant Nescafé from the Red Cross food parcel, stirred it into the hot water, and presto! He had precious coffee to distribute to everyone in his car. Then he turned his attention to the young typhoid patient, lying on the makeshift stretcher suspended from the two overhead luggage racks. He took some morsels of bread and dipped them into the coffee to soften them, then tenderly fed it to the listless young typhoid patient. After a few mouthfuls, the young man opened his eyes and whispered hoarsely, "Mr. Springer, you saved my life."

Mr. Springer then took some dried milk powder and a piece of honey cake from the priceless Red Cross package and mixed it with the coffee. Then, with much patience and devotion, he literally forced it into the mouth of the forty-year-old man who did not have the strength to hold his head up. As the hot, sweet liquid entered the sick man's mouth, a spark of life returned to his eyes. Mr. Springer continued spooning the sweet concoction into the man's mouth until he indicated that he had had enough. Mr. Springer would recall time and again, many years later, how the satisfaction and delight that he felt upon hearing the sigh of contentment that escaped that man's lips remained engraved in his heart forever.

They already had refreshments, they had already saved two people from imminent death, and they were still stranded on this motionless train. What was going on?

Eventually, they were given another meal of bread and cheese. Those who could ate until their hunger was satisfied. But they still couldn't satisfy the niggling question of why the train wasn't moving.

One theory bandied about was that the train might be stranded because of the heavy bombardment by the Allied Forces in the area. Perhaps the railway tracks had been bombed, and the train would never be able to go anywhere.

Mr. Springer, however, was immune to the impatience and frustration of his fellow passengers. After all, he had saved the lives of two people. He fervently hoped that they would both live to experience total freedom and go on to lead happy, productive lives, but who was to know? His guess was that the young man who had typhoid had better odds of survival than the forty-year-old with only the Red Cross food parcel to keep him alive. He had done his part, and the rest was up to Hashem.

A Mensch in All Circumstances

After a meal of bread and cheese, everyone was desperately thirsty. Mr. Springer once again approached the guard for permission to bring some water to the parched prisoners. When permission was granted, it once again fell to the ever-forthcoming Mr. Springer to make the trek to the nearby structure. Before long, he was back with a huge bucket of hot water.

Like before, everyone handed him their coffee packets from the Red Cross parcels, and Mr. Springer duly mixed them into the bucket of water—soon everyone was sipping hot coffee. And as he had done in the morning, Mr. Springer soon turned his attention to the two infirm men—the forty-year-old and the young typhoid patient. Thankfully, both were doing much better but were still in no condition to be able to eat or drink independently. Mr. Springer fed them both with the utmost care and devotion.

But it was not destined for Mr. Springer to rest on his laurels—even after lugging in heavy pails of water for his car mates and tending so solicitously to the two ill patients. Much to his horror, he noticed that several more patients fell ill and were feverish. One of them had such high temperature that he was incoherent. Two things made matters worse: One, that this man was extremely tall, and it was a major challenge to place him in a laying position. And two, as if that wasn't enough, he also had a very tough, uncompromising temperament, which was exacerbated by his illness, and he wouldn't cooperate with those who wanted to help him.

The stench in the train became ever worse, and the passengers became increasingly restless. Mr. Springer, desperate to maintain order and harmony at all costs, directed his car mates to change places once again. But the tall, feverish patient refused to budge, giving Mr. Springer, who really wanted to help him, a huge headache.

It was a mixed blessing that no one in Mr. Springer's car died. While this was of course truly great, the downside was that unlike in other cars—where many people succumbed to illness, and their bodies were unceremoniously flung out of the train, leaving the survivors with more space—Mr. Springer's car remained very crowded. This was likely due to Mr. Springer's and Leibish's painstaking efforts to keep order and help their fellow passengers survive.

Glancing out the window, Mr. Springer's gaze fell on the piles of dead bodies lying next to mounds of human excrement. He felt that this was a reprehensible sight and terribly degrading to the deceased. It disturbed him greatly. He felt that it was only a matter of time, and he might be lying among them.

But ultimately, he took hold of his emotions and willed himself to think positively. The last six years had been all torture and darkness with nary a ray of sunshine in sight. But there finally were some rays of hope, such as the arrival of the Red Cross parcels. Wasn't this a sign from Heaven that their salvation was imminent?

In the meantime, Mr. Springer's immediate concern was dealing with the tall sick man. Leibish tried to help Mr. Springer arrange a spot for the lanky patient to no avail. Finally, Leibish came up with a brainstorm that left Mr. Springer awestruck. What if Leibish vacated his seat and went to stand by the door? That seat would then become available for the tall patient. Mr. Springer was moved to tears by the selflessness and *middos* of this young teenager who displayed such character at a time when others in his circumstances were exhibiting the most selfish, animalistic traits. Mr. Springer was no less proud of him than he would have been of his own son!

As Leibish was standing by the door, he noticed the Hungarian guard there and proceeded to strike up a conversation with him. Mr. Springer soon joined them, which freed up his seat as well. So it became a bit roomier and airier, and spirits became a bit lighter as well.

As the two friends, Leibish and Mr. Springer, stood by the door, Leibish noticed the familiar dreamy look on the older man's face, followed by a blissful smile that settled on his countenance. "What's going on, Mr. Springer?" Leibish prodded him. "Are you hallucinating once again? I hope you don't have any fever."

"No, no. Don't worry," Mr. Springer reassured Leibish. "I just decided to mentally escape this hellhole. I let my mind dwell on past and, hopefully, future pleasures. I find this very helpful in dealing with the misery of our current reality." Looking at Leibish pitifully, he continued, "You are still young and never experienced any other kind of life than that in your parents' house. Therefore, you can't even fathom the pleasures that life has to offer. If you could, you would also be able to mentally escape these miserable conditions."

Leibish, however, did not need to resort to fantasies of future pleasures. For him the emuna and bitachon that he absorbed in his parents' home was enough to keep him strong and optimistic that better times were coming.

Leibish kept on checking up on his three ill car mates and doing whatever he could to make them more comfortable. Unlike so many other concentration camp sufferers who had become cold and unfeeling to others, Leibish remained kind-hearted and compassionate, always prepared to help out someone in need.

Seeing that there was still no locomotive in sight and the train was not going anywhere soon, Leibish urged Mr. Springer to appeal to the guard and ask him for permission to place the sick men in the corridor, leaving a bit more room in the train for the others.

Derision for the Living, Disdain for the Dead

Leibish had risen from his seat to go stand by the door, his intention being to create a little more room for others. But that little gesture was the precursor to something even better.

When Leibish conversed with the Hungarian guard in their mutual mother tongue, the latter was somewhat disarmed. But when Mr. Springer approached him with a request to place the three sick men in the corridor, he refused. Mr. Springer was crestfallen. Then Leibish spoke to him, appealing to him as "one Magyar to another." He begged him to allow the three infirm men be allowed to lie in the corridor during the day while it was still light. This way the crowding would be somewhat alleviated during the day. He added that the three patients were so sick and feeble that there was no need to worry that they would attempt to escape.

The Hungarian guard considered Leibish's request and agreed to let the three men be placed in the corridor during the daytime hours. This provided significant relief to all the others in the car, each of whom had a bit more room now. As dusk approached, Leibish mustered the courage to speak to the guard again and cajole him into allowing the three sick men to stay where they were all night as well. Initially, the guard resisted, claiming that in the darkness they were at risk of being trampled on by others. However, Leibish did not let up and eventually he prevailed.

Everyone hoped that night would be more comfortable than the previous one. But, alas, it was not to be. In fact, it was even more chaotic than the night before, with one out of three people suddenly afflicted with diarrhea. The single metal bucket that was supposed to serve the elimination needs of the entire car was painfully inadequate. Despite how quickly the bucket was passed from one to the other, it was not quick enough. Desperate attempts to empty the bucket out the windows in the darkness yielded disastrous results. No one could see where they were going and where they were treading. The situation became more and more unbearable with each passing minute. Even though the three ill men were now in the corridor, the car was still terribly overcrowded. Many people developed painful leg cramps, and their cries of agony reverberated through the car. Mr. Springer tried valiantly to restore some order, calling for the men to rotate places as originally agreed. However, no one wanted to budge, partly because they didn't know what they would be stepping into. Unlike the previous night when they managed to get at least some sleep, that night, not even a wink.

Adding even more to their misery was that the excessive human waste that was dumped outside the train attracted hordes of flies, which then swarmed in through the broken windows, stinging and biting the wretched men.

Mr. Springer realized that the situation had reached a new unbearable low, and all of his directives would fall on deaf ears. So he changed his tone and tried coaxing and wheedling his comrades into better spirits.

"Look here," he implored them. "You know the war is almost over. If the Germans wanted to kill us, they would have done so a while ago. The reason they are not killing us is that they know they are losing the war. This means that our troubles are about to end." Mr. Springer made another noteworthy observation: "This train station is definitely a target of Allied Force bombardment. Just look at all the missile batteries the Germans have set up, knowing that this area is targeted. We can hear the bombs falling nearby, but none have fallen on this station. Don't you see that Heaven is helping us?"

But try as he might, Mr. Springer failed to calm the overwrought temperaments. Chaos and tension prevailed throughout the night. When Thursday morning dawned, they made the somber discovery that two people in the car had died. Stepping over frail, sick people was one thing; treading on deceased people was gut-wrenching. It wasn't as if they weren't used to the sight of dead people. They had seen plenty in the camps. But having to trample them was something else, and the indignity of it shook them to the core. Their despair was boundless.

Mr. Springer's Wise Rebuke

Predictably, everyone was run down and malnourished and some people were seriously ill. Yet both Leibish and Mr. Springer did not suffer from typhus or dysentery like so many others did. They were also much stronger emotionally and morally than most others. There was one particular man in the railcar with them who was tall, broadly built, and relatively robust. Unfortunately, the years of pain and suffering in inhuman conditions hardened him and brought out his most animalistic tendencies. When he saw that some people in his car were gravely ill, he simply helped himself to their Red Cross parcels, having already eaten the contents of his own parcel.

Mr. Springer was horrified and outraged that someone could stoop so low, and he severely reprimanded the villain, threatening that if he ever dared take anything from someone else again, Mr. Springer would report the man to the Germans—something he was really loath to do. Moreover, the next time food would be distributed, this rascal would be expected to use half of his loaf to reimburse those poor people from whom he had stolen. The reprobate hung his head in shame and agreed to give half of his next loaf to Mr. Springer for him to dispense as he saw fit. Mr. Springer continued to feel a sense of responsibility for his car mates. He once again appealed to the guard and asked for permission to leave the train to go fetch water, so he could make coffee for his dehydrated comrades. The guard agreed to let Mr. Springer go, and even suggested that he take along a volunteer to help him carry the water. Mr. Springer made an announcement, asking for a volunteer, but none was forthcoming. Even Leibish, who was usually the first to volunteer his services, did not feel up to the task this time.

Suddenly, the man Mr. Springer had just reprimanded for stealing food, called out, "I don't mind going with you. I will help you bring the water." If Mr. Springer was surprised, he didn't show it. He wisely used the opportunity as a teaching moment, speaking gently to the man: "I know that you are an inherently good person. Surely your moral lapse was only due to the terrible trials and tribulations you've been through. The Nazi fiends have succeeded in stripping too many people of their humanity. You have to retrieve your lost humanity and realize that you are a person of worth and dignity, regardless of what the German barbarians have done to us."

Mr. Springer continued to speak kindly and encouragingly to the man, telling him that obviously when someone dies, it is acceptable to take whatever is left of his food parcel, but it is never acceptable to take something away from someone while he is alive.

Mr. Springer and his companion filled up the bucket with water, heated it, and brought it back to their parched comrades. At 9:00 a.m., parcels of bread and cheese were distributed. Although the former miscreant now realized that he had erred in his ways, Mr. Springer still insisted on taking half of his loaf and dividing it between the two people he had wronged.

One of the men whose food had been seized was now almost on the verge of death. He motioned for Mr. Springer to bend over him, so he could tell him something. "Look," the ill man whispered. "I'm too sick to eat. But that man there," he pointed to the man who had taken his food parcel, "he is probably starving. Let him have the bread." Mr. Springer was extremely moved by the man's nobility of spirit. "See," he said to the former wrongdoer. "Look at the value and dignity that a human being can possess. In the last moments of his life, he is thinking of you and your needs. Who knows what time has in store for us? Life is so fleeting. At least while we're alive, we have to think of others and conduct ourselves with fairness and dignity."

The man listened to Mr. Springer and seemed genuinely contrite. Leibish, who had been privy to the entire conversation, exclaimed, "Wow, Mr. Springer, you sound just like my father! This was always his message to his children."

Mr. Springer looked at Leibish affectionately. He knew that Leibish was raised in a warm, loving, stable, principled home and missed his parents dreadfully. Although Leibish still harbored hope that his mother was still alive, Mr.

Springer knew better. He knew that the odds of Leibish ever seeing either of his parents were practically nil. "Luckily, we have each other," he said to Leibish encouragingly. Both broke into tears as they continued to hope and wait for their deliverance from this hellhole.

Later that morning, some good news finally arrived. At 7:00 p.m. that day, the train would finally be leaving this place where they had endured so much suffering. The tortured souls did not know what to make of this news. Dare they believe that they really would be leaving the hordes of insects, the unbearable stench, the disease, the piles of dead bodies, and last but not least, the danger of a bomb landing atop their train?

While most passengers allowed themselves to be cautiously optimistic about the upcoming journey, Mr. Springer, as he was prone to doing, fell into his state of a sort of self-hypnosis where he basked in his own private sphere of pleasure, worlds away from his surroundings.

When Mr. Springer offered to take Leibish along on his journey to fantasy land, Leibish waved him away. He didn't need to resort to fantasy and hallucinations to achieve serenity. He had his emuna and bitachon intact, believing that Hashem would soon dispel the darkness and shine the light of peace and liberation on them. He shared his thoughts with Mr. Springer who drew much inspiration from them.

Thoughts of the impending liberation were poignantly bittersweet for the two comrades in misery. Both knew instinctively that as soon as normalcy returned to their world, their paths in life would diverge, and they would inevitably go their separate ways.

While news of the forthcoming journey was indeed very exhilarating, it did nothing to slake their thirst. By noon, the passengers were begging Mr. Springer to try and obtain permission to go and fetch some water. But this time, the guard categorically refused since they were "leaving very soon." Mr. Springer regretfully told the passengers that this time he was unable to help them.

In the meantime, the sick man (the one who had his food parcel taken from him) took a turn for the worse. Mr. Springer felt terrible that he didn't have a drop of water to offer the man. Rummaging through his own food parcel, Mr. Springer withdrew some food and tried feeding it to the man, but he indicated that he was too weak and couldn't ingest anything.

It was quite apparent that this man was dying. Mr. Springer spoke quietly to the two men sitting near him and implored them to move over a bit so that the sick man might die in a more comfortable position. Then Mr. Springer and one other kindly volunteer gave up their seats and remained standing. The sick man was then stretched out across the space of three seats, and within a short time, his soul departed to a better world.

Although he was but a sixteen-year-old lad, Leibish possessed a maturity and sense of responsibility way beyond his years—the kind that only extreme hardship and suffering bring. As he looked around at his weary, parched car mates, he was struck with an idea. Approaching the guard, he entreated him, "Look, you say that we can't go and bring water, but please allow us to alight from the train and walk around for a bit—just to stretch our limbs and to shake the lice and insects off our clothes." Surprisingly, the guard agreed, and the men gratefully shuffled off the train. They removed their clothes and shook off the ubiquitous crawling, buzzing insects, and they felt better…for a very short time. Before long, the banished insects were replaced by droves of newly arrived insects that swarmed all over them with a vengeance, until the very bread they ate was infested with them.

Many years later, in happier times, when Leibish would recall the plague of Kinim at the Pesach Seder, it was not just an abstract recital, but a very real, powerful flashback to the hordes of flying, crawling pests that overtook them as they languished in that train.

While they were absorbed in picking the lice off their clothes and chasing the swarms of pests off their bodies, an announcement came over the loud-speaker: "*Achtung! Achtung!* Everyone should to return to their place on the train immediately! An Appell will be conducted shortly." There hadn't been an Appell since they passed through the gates of Dachau. The Jews lost no time in obeying the command. As soon as they returned to their places on the train, a head count was conducted. Only the Nazi guards knew how many passengers had boarded the train two days ago and how many of them were still alive. It had been two days—from Tuesday, April 24 until Thursday, April 26—but to the poor, battered Jews it seemed like an eternity. The piles of dead bodies outside the train spoke volumes, even without the head count.

The Train Is Finally Moving

Finally, at 6:00 p.m., the shrill tooting of a locomotive filled the air. To the Jews, this was the most beautiful sound in the world. Within ten minutes the train was attached to the locomotive, and the train started moving. The relief in the air was palpable. But their relief was tinged with anxiety. Who knew where they were being taken? To be shot? Gassed? Or…maybe to freedom? All they could do was hope for the best.

Although the train was finally moving, the conditions in the car were still horrendous. Diarrhea was rampant, and the malodorous bucket could not be passed along quickly enough. Disposal was accomplished by heaving the contents of the bucket out the window of the moving train, which typically yielded some very unpleasant results.

The train chugged along all night. Leibish and Mr. Springer stood by the door so that the other passengers might have some more room. Eventually, Leibish felt exhausted and looked around for a place to sit down. But the situation had gone from bad to worse, and many people died throughout the night. Sadly, at that point it was not even possible to lay the dying people down, so they could die with some semblance of dignity. They were forced to remain upright even in death.

Now, even Leibish and Mr. Springer, the two most stalwart of the group, were on the verge of breaking down. They had no strength left to stand, there was no room for them to sit, and they couldn't even budge for fear of stepping on dead bodies. Suddenly, Leibish burst into sobs. "How much longer? Will this ever end?" Although Mr. Springer was also filled with despair, he mustered the inner strength to encourage his young friend.

"See how slow the train is going? This is because the Allied Forces are close by. Surely, we'll be liberated real soon. Looks like we're headed to Munich. That's good news because then we'll be in Allied hands. Even if the train will pass Munich and not stop, there are Allied Forces throughout the area who would liberate us. Leibish, now is not the time to give up. We're almost there!"

The train continued on throughout Thursday night. Friday at dawn, glancing out the windows, they saw bombed villages, houses destroyed, devastation everywhere. "Wow!" Leibish exclaimed, "we can see villages."

Mr. Springer explained, "This must be Munich. Apparently, the Allied Forces have not captured the city yet. There are still ongoing skirmishes." The train did not stop in Munich and continued on toward the south of Germany, away from the battle scenes and bombardment, with the intended destination of Austria.

The passengers tried guessing and speculating as to their destination. Some ventured a guess that maybe they were being taken to Switzerland, per the old rumors back in Dachau.

The train got to a stretch of unused, out-of-the-way tracks and lurched to a stop. The guards alighted from the train to see what was going on, but they would not let any of the passengers disembark. The passengers were to stay put in the reeking, squalid car, surrounded by dead and dying bodies, without any food or water.

Realizing that the train had come to a full stop, the beleaguered Jews experienced a sudden flow of adrenalin, and with incredible alacrity, they began hauling the dead bodies out of the train and onto the tracks. This didn't sit well with the SS guards' sensibilities, and they protested vehemently. "Hey, what do you think you're doing? You can't just dump dead bodies on the railroad tracks!" But the long-suffering Jews were fed up with the Nazis telling them what they could and couldn't do. Perhaps it was the thought of their imminent liberation that emboldened them. Even Mr. Springer, who had always been so intent on keeping the peace, was also feeling angry and rebellious.

The incredible fact was that the Jews simply ignored the Germans' objections and continued removing the dead bodies from the car.

Ironically, it was the young sixteen-year-old Leibish who had the maturity and wisdom to put a lid on the simmering tempers. Pulling Mr. Springer aside, Leibish spoke to him quietly and rationally: "Weren't you just telling me how sure you are that the war is almost over, and we'll soon be free? We've already been through so much. Let's just be patient a little bit longer." Mr. Springer saw the veracity of Leibish's words and accordingly turned to the passengers and persuaded them to keep calm and try to not provoke the SS guards.

The train soon continued on until it came to a freight station where it stopped so that the SS guards could use the facilities and also pick up some food. The SS allowed two kapos, accompanied by two inmates, to take a blanket in which they wrapped some bread to bring back to the train. Every person got one quarter of a loaf of bread. There was no water or anything to drink. The Hungarian guard whom Leibish had befriended told them that they would soon be arriving to a conventional train station where they could get water, and there they would also be able to dispose of the many dead bodies still left in the train.

Leibish and Mr. Springer, detecting a note of goodwill in the Hungarian guard's voice, decided to press their luck. As long as the train was standing motionless, perhaps the long-restricted Jews could be allowed to disembark from the train to shake the lice out of their clothes and to brush off some of the filth that had accumulated on them. When permission was granted, it brought some much-needed relief to the rundown, half-dead passengers.

The train soon resumed her tedious journey, and just as the Hungarian guard had predicted, it eventually pulled into a proper train station where permission was officially granted for the removal of all the corpses. The mere sight of so many dead bodies was dispiriting. However, as incredible and revolting as the thought may seem today, there was also a sense of relief, knowing that they would benefit from the extra space that would now be available to them. They would no longer have to sit shoulder to shoulder with dead bodies.

It turned out, though, that the Hungarian guard's promise of water was not borne out; there was none to be had at this station. The train lumbered along at a snail's pace while the parched passengers became more and more restless and desperate for a drink. The guards sent a message to the conductor that he would have to stop somewhere soon for desperately needed water. Very shortly after, the train came to a stop and several passengers from each car were allowed off the train. But first they had to rinse the bucket (yes, the aforementioned bucket) to bring back water.

It turned out that the water was ice cold; cold water is known to exacerbate dysentery and diarrhea, which plagued so many of the passengers. However, most of them did not have the mental fortitude to resist the cold water and drank their fill. Mr. Springer was more wary and duly enjoined Leibish from drinking the cold water.

The train ended up staying there for several hours, until late at night. All too soon, the cold water began to wreak its treacherous results on the passengers. Everyone's diarrhea worsened, and many of them died. Of the original twenty passengers in Mr. Springer's car, only fifteen remained. The other cars had even fewer surviving passengers since people had been dying in them from the beginning of the journey.

Mr. Springer suggested to Leibish that he ask his "landsman," the Hungarian guard, to allow some passengers from their car be transferred to other cars that were less crowded. The guard agreed, and two passengers were duly relocated to other cars, leaving the car somewhat roomier, so passengers could actually try and get some sleep. In middle of the night, some passengers heard the sounds of people singing. Peering out the window, they saw some houses, people, and life. All signs of normal life. How exhilarating!

In the darkness, the passengers were able to make out an open freight train loaded with sugar cane standing not far from their train. Disregarding the fact that they were officially prohibited from disembarking without express permission from the guards, one passenger after another snuck off the train and, under the cover of darkness, sidled up to the freight train where they scooped up piles of sugar cane, which they surreptitiously shared with all the people on the train. This happened to be Friday night, and it was the first time in a very long time that the Jews had experienced such a "sweet" *oneg* Shabbos!

In the morning, the guards must have noticed some telltale signs of the passengers' nocturnal escapade, and the proclamation was not long in coming: anyone who would dare get off the train would be summarily shot. Notably, there was some uncertainty among the passengers as to whether their guards were fully armed. On the one hand, they exhibited some measure of laxity compared to their trigger-happy reign in Dachau. Yet no one knew for sure that they were unarmed; hence, they were still vulnerable to threats of being shot.

Later some bread, margarine, and cheese were passed out. The train remained motionless until Shabbos afternoon. Then someone announced the news, which was later confirmed, that the passengers were not being taken to Switzerland but to Tyrol in the alps of Austria, near the German border.

This was very disheartening news. Is this what they had survived Dachau for? All the suffering and squalor they had endured on the hellish train ride, only to be transferred to yet another concentration camp? Panicked sobs, anguished thoughts, heavy hearts—none of it helped them in their dire straits. The train continued on relentlessly until it reached the village of Seefeld in Tyrol.

This marked the end of the tragic chapter that was the train ride out of Dachau, which was arguably a continuation of the horrendous carnage they were subjected to in Dachau.

Years later when Leibish would recount his harrowing experiences in the concentration camps, he would deliberately omit the appalling details of that train ride. He knew that that would be beyond the scope of the comprehension for people in a normal, civilized world. Anyone with the barest modicum of decency would be absolutely revolted by even a fraction of what transpired on that train. Still, it is important for those fortunate enough to be born in a different world, in a different era, to realize the depths of ferocious depravity so-called human beings, actually German fiends, were capable of.

Mr. Springer wrote in his memoirs many years later that the horror and trauma of that train ride haunted him all his life, and he could never rid himself of its sinister aftereffects.

CHAPTER 8

Last Leg of SS Control

Still More Suffering

IN SEEFELD THE SS officers ordered the half-dead Jews to form a column and prepare for a march. The local police arrived with trucks on which they loaded all the (many) dead bodies and carted them off for unceremonious disposal. Sadly, even the survivors of that ride were more dead than alive. When they heard that they were to embark on a march, they were devastated. After the Gehinnom they had endured on the train, not even counting what they had been through in Dachau, they were certainly in no position to march anywhere.

The bestial Nazis were not deterred. Even though the "glorious" Third Reich was already in her death throes, they still held the long-suffering Jews in their ruthless iron grip and under their hobnailed boots. And if they decreed that the Jews would march to some unknown destination, then that's exactly what they would have to do—regardless of their weak, debilitated conditions.

And so the feeble, barely alive Jews propped each other up and dragged each other along so that they could obey the Nazis' orders to "march," fully aware of what would be the consequences of refusal/inability to march.

If they thought, as they trudged pathetically through the idyllic village of Seefeld, that they would find some sympathy in the local populace, they were sadly mistaken. On the contrary, all the pure-blooded Aryan inhabitants they passed looked at them coldly, with obvious disdain and contempt in their eyes, as if the Jews were the criminals!

When they arrived at the outskirts of the village, the SS guards issued the next command: the whacked-out Jews were now to clamber up the tall, steep mountains, surrounded by undergrowth and shrubbery, where snow and ice were still commonplace at the end of April. Predictably, very few of the knocked-out Jews succeeded in making it to the top of the mountain, and all too many dropped from sheer exhaustion and were left to die.

Both Leibish and Mr. Springer would forever retain the gruesome images of the frail, weary, and sick Jews imploring the Nazi guards to shoot them and put them out of their misery. The Nazi brutes, however, wouldn't waste a bullet on them.

In truth the guards themselves were also exhausted from the whole ordeal. They felt that their control over the prisoners was slipping away, and some prisoners with enough guts managed to "get lost" in the woodland. Most of them were both too weak and too fearful to take this step. After all, they didn't know for sure whether the Nazi brutes still had their weapons. Huddling with the commandants, the guards tried to convince them to allow an about-face and return to the village. But the commandants would not hear of it.

After a long and arduous trek, they (those who survived) arrived at a village high up on the mountain. Years later when they would recall that brutal trek, Mr. Springer and Leibish always marveled anew at how they, or any of their fellow prisoners, made it all the way up that steep mountain. Clearly, there is no logical explanation for that impossible feat.

There at the summit, every SS guard was responsible for a group of prisoners for whom he was expected to find a place where they could bed down. Some groups were "lucky," and their guard promptly found a spot and some bundles of hay. They could lie down straightaway. Mr. Springer and Leibish's group were not so lucky, and it took their guard quite a while to locate a deserted barn, albeit one without any hay or straw—just a dirt floor. It was cold and dark, and a chilly mountain wind howled through the cracks. Try as they might, they couldn't find a comfortable spot. Eventually, their bone-weary exhaustion got the better of them, and they dozed off on the cold dirt floor.

Not long after he drifted into a fitful sleep, Mr. Springer woke with a start. Apparently, he had caught a draft from the chilly winds that raged throughout the ramshackle barn, and his right side was stiff and sore. He could not move his right arm at all. Understandably, his distress was boundless. Here he was, high atop a cold, steep mountain, totally incapacitated. He was worse off here than he had been in Dachau.

Leibish was deeply affected by this newest calamity that had befallen Mr. Springer, who had cared for him and helped him in such a fatherly fashion. Leibish cut up Mr. Springer's bread for him and sobbed out loud to see his friend and benefactor in such a state.

As soon as the sun's rays filtered in through the slats in the roof, the Jews went outside the decrepit barn, hoping to warm up in the sunshine. To quench their burning thirst, they scooped up handfuls of snow, which they gulped down. Suddenly, they heard a sonorous proclamation from the SS guards: "Achtung, everyone! We're going back down the mountain and heading back to Seefeld."

This was truly beyond belief! Such an exercise in futility—to make them clamber up the steep mountain, only to have them descend as soon as they got there. But as upset and shattered as they were, they were still in the clutches of the wicked SS and were still terrified of them. And so, barely able to put one foot in front of the other, they began the trek down the mountain. On the way, they came across many of the corpses of the hapless people who had died on the way up. Looking around, they came to the disheartening realization that half of their group that had left Dachau was no longer alive.

Leibish was extremely weak, especially after another sleepless night; he could not even keep his balance or stand up straight. Because of this, Mr. Springer, whose right arm was paralyzed, supported Leibish and pulled him along with his left arm. In this manner they dragged themselves back down the mountain. Later when they were finally liberated, a doctor's examination proved that Leibish was much weaker and more underweight than Mr. Springer was.

In Seefeld they stopped at the train station where they were given a quarter of a loaf of soggy bread, which they devoured ravenously. But once again they found themselves plagued by a burning thirst. Some desperate Jews simply knocked on the doors of some local villagers and were lucky enough to get some water. Leibish and Mr. Springer made do with drops of rainwater that they managed to find.

No one knew what would happen next. In fact, they didn't even know what had gone on during the past twenty-four hours. What was the purpose of taking them up the mountain, only to bring them back down? Only much later did they discover the sobering truth behind this mystery. The SS guards had received orders from their higher-ups to "get rid" of the surviving Jews. That is why they were led through the woods and up the mountain. That would be an ideal setting to shoot them all. But for some unknown reason, the SS guards decided at the last minute not to carry out the shootings.

It is reasonable to surmise that the SS guards felt that the Allied Forces were too close by, and they would not have the opportunity to cover their tracks.

Before the Jews left Seefeld, they experienced a relatively insignificant incident that gave them an inkling about the attitudes and feelings of the general Austrian-German population. Clearly, the ruthless, hateful anti-Semitism that the SS, Gestapo, and Nazis personified was just as rampant among all segments of the population.

It was Sunday morning, April 29. Although the calendar might have proclaimed springtime, the actual temperatures in the Alps were still very cold. The sickly Jews shivered from the cold, which penetrated their very bones. They wanted to light a bonfire to warm up a bit. But very shortly after, the mayor of the village came running and sternly commanded that the fire be immediately extinguished since the smoke might be harmful to the livestock.

One look at the emaciated, freezing Jews should have been enough to melt a heart of stone. The fire they had lit was small and well-contained. But the mayor remained adamant. The fire had to be extinguished immediately. He was taking no chances with the villagers' livestock. The ill-concealed contempt in his eyes spoke volumes. Clearly, in his mind the livestock ranked higher than the gaunt, starving, sickly Jews.

In the afternoon, the Jews were once again given bread and cheese. And the interminable wait continued. Although they knew they were on the cusp of liberation by the Americans, the Jews were fearful and anxious. Who could know what evil designs the Germans still had in store for them before the Americans would arrive?

Several hours later, the weary Jews were made to stand up for a head count. After enduring the miserable Appells twice daily for the duration of their stay in the concentration camp, this was the last time they were made to go through this tedious ordeal. Each guard was assigned to a group of Jews for whom he was responsible. While they were still being counted, a train that consisted of three cargo cars and a locomotive came hurtling into the station.

The SS guards announced that the train would serve as a shuttle that would transport them. Where to? That was anyone's guess. Also, there was clearly not enough room on the train for all the passengers, which is why they made it a shuttle. One group after another was loaded onto the three cars, and the train whisked them away. It then returned to the station about forty-five minutes later to transport the remaining Jews.

Seeing the empty cars of the returning train was truly a frightening sight for the Jews who remained waiting at the station. Where had the Jews from the previous transports been taken? Leibish and Mr. Springer decided that they would stick together, come what may. They would insist on boarding the train together and would disembark together. And if it meant remaining in Seefeld, then so be it. They would not be separated.

When it was their turn to board the train, there were about two or three hundred Jews remaining in Seefeld. Theirs turned out to be the last shuttle out of Seefeld. Leibish and Mr. Springer never learned the fate of the few hundred Jews who remained in Seefeld.

Liberated!

The shuttle traveled some distance and eventually came to a stop in middle of the tracks. Looking out the window, they saw mountains on one side and a stream on the other. Between the mountains and the stream was an open field where they spotted the passengers from the previous shuttle standing around, waiting for them. This was very encouraging. At least they were alive. This could only mean that this seemingly endless war was finally over and with it the arbitrary killing of Jews. Mr. Springer's thoughts began racing. The guards, though present, seemed to be rather distracted. Should they make an attempt to slink away and return to Seefeld which was, after all, a populated village, as opposed to this desolate wilderness?

In the meantime, though, Mr. Springer and Leibish opted to bide their time and remain with the others. In view of their apparent isolation from any civilization, they ventured to build a bonfire to warm up. But almost instantly the sounds of gunshots could be heard from the mountains, which they understood as a warning that the fire was to be immediately extinguished. Apparently, they weren't as isolated from the outside world as it seemed.

Night fell and the weary wanderers began foraging around for some rocks that might afford them some meager protection against the wind and cold. Covering themselves with some rags and tatters, they tried to get some sleep. But, as luck would have it, in middle of the night, a heavy snowfall combined with a deluge of rain dispelled any hope of sleep and gave them a freezing and thorough drenching.

But even in this sorry state, their exhaustion got the better of them, and incredibly, they drifted off into some sort of sleep. It was in the midst of this state of half-asleep and half-awake that Mr. Springer suddenly bolted upright with an electrified awareness of something unusual. Glancing around, he was struck by the absence of the SS guards. Not believing his eyes, he nudged Leibish awake. "Leibish, I'm not sure of what I'm seeing. Please look around and tell me if you see the Nazi guards anywhere."

Leibish duly rose to his knees and looked around groggily. Sure enough, there were no guards in sight. Before long the word spread among the stunned "no longer" prisoners. The guards had disappeared! It took a while for this new development to sink in. When it did, Mr. Springer's first inclination was to once again light a fire to dry them after the night's downpour. Leibish, however, was hesitant. He remembered only too well the reaction generated by the fire they tried to build earlier.

But while Leibish and Mr. Springer were debating the issue, some other brave souls had already come to a decision and were already busy building a fire. The group held their collective breath as they looked around anxiously, but thankfully, there were no more gunshots directed at them. Nor were there any signs of soldiers, guards, or officers of any kind. It was as if they were on a different planet that was inhabited only by skeletal, starved, and debilitated Muselmänner. This encouraged them to scavenge for more scraps of wood to enhance the fire until they were all warm and dry.

Eventually they got around to heating some water as well. Mr. Springer miraculously produced a packet of instant coffee that he had managed to salvage. He rinsed a bowl in which he subsequently boiled water, and, voilà, there was "coffee" for everyone. Truth be told, the "coffee" probably contained coffee, coals, and dirt in equal proportions; still, no one complained as it served to warm their hands, stomachs, and hearts simultaneously.

Slowly, the long-suffering, shattered Jews processed the incredibly amazing realization that they were indeed free men. At the crack of dawn, as soon as there was a ray of sunlight, the former prisoners set out on their march to freedom.

CHAPTER 9

Wandering in the Wilderness

Still a Long Way from Home

LEIBISH WAS EXCEEDINGLY WEAK, while Mr. Springer's arm was still stiff and quite useless. However, their boost in spirits spawned a boost in overall strength, which enabled them to set one foot in front of the other as they leaned on each other for support. The last time food was distributed by the SS was actually while they were stranded idling on the horrific train. With miraculous Divine intervention, they stopped at the first house they came across and knocked on the door. The woman who opened the door did not need to ask what they wanted. The ravenous hunger in their eyes said it all. She brought out some old bread, which seemed like a veritable feast to the starving men.

Indeed, Leibish and Mr. Springer were strengthened and rejuvenated, and their ability to walk independently was improved. They continued their trek until the next farmhouse where they also knocked on the door. The woman who answered their knock was appalled by their unkempt, half-dead appearance and immediately put up a pot of milk to boil. This "delicacy" warmed their bodies and quite literally restored some life into their souls.

It was Monday, April 30, 1945. By this time the sun had risen in all her splendor, and the glorious rays warmed the hearts and raised the spirits of the newly liberated Jews. Now that they were free and had finally internalized that fact, their thoughts turned to their families from whom they had been so brutally torn asunder. Mr. Springer kept wondering out loud, "Dare I hope to find my wife? Perhaps my children are still alive? At least one of them?" Leibish dreamed of being reunited with his parents and siblings.

Suddenly, an SS officer appeared in the distance and headed straight toward them. Brandishing his rifle, he hissed, "Back off, you criminal lowlifes! Where do you think you're going? Go back where you came from!" Leibish and Mr. Springer froze in terror as the Nazi strode toward them, rifle cocked. But much to their relief, he just sauntered right past them without harming them.

After their hearts had stopped pounding, they tried to figure out what this encounter was about. Was the Nazi perhaps fearful that the two Jews would want to exact revenge and attack him? Maybe with the "glorious" Third Reich in its death throes, he just wanted to get in some last licks of terrorizing some wretched Jewish vagrants. Clearly, though, he had much more to fear from the Americans than the Jews from him.

Leibish and Mr. Springer continued their arduous trek up and down steep mountains. Wanting to avoid main roads and thoroughfares for fear of encountering SS men, they preferred to traverse muddy hills and valleys.

After a while of not encountering any Nazis, Mr. Springer deemed it safe to approach the easier-to-navigate roads. "Let's just keep to the side of the road since the center is more likely to contain mines."

They didn't even realize when they crossed the border from Austria into Germany and reached the mountainous terrain surrounding the city of Mittenwald. Taking advantage of the radiant sunshine, they sat down to bask in her warm rays. They also tried to rid themselves of the flying, crawling insects that were all over their bodies.

As they passed one village after another, Leibish ventured to Mr. Springer that perhaps they should muster the guts to knock on the door of one of the houses and ask to be allowed to sleep in a bed. But if they thought liberation from the death camps would garner some sympathy from the local residents, they were quickly disillusioned when one villager after another coldly and contemptuously shooed them away as if they were indeed lowlife criminals. They were not even allowed to sleep in a barn.

And so, with their last bit of strength, they staggered along until they saw the city of Mittenwald at the foot of the mountain. They gazed in awe at the houses and streets that were teeming with people. Slowly and with much difficulty, they made the grueling descent down. When they were halfway down, they were able to make out figures like themselves, wearing the striped concentration camp uniforms and walking around freely. Leibish and Mr. Springer found this very encouraging.

By this time Leibish was so spent that he could hardly put one foot in front of the other, but the heartening signs of life in front of them prompted a surge of adrenalin that enabled him to persevere. When they reached the edge of the village, they were elated to see that this was no illusion; there were actually other Jewish former inmates there who directed them to go down to the end of a winding road where there was an impressive-looking hotel that was serving free meals to refugees.

Leaning on each other, the two comrades made the laborious trek to the courtyard and asked where they might get some food. They were informed that all they needed to do was go up two flights of stairs, and they would find themselves in the dining room where nourishing meals were indeed available. However, as far as Leibish and Mr. Springer were concerned, this was easier said than done. After all they had been through, they were totally sapped and could not muster the strength to clamber up two flights of stairs—even with proper nourishing food as an incentive.

As they were standing there dejectedly, they were approached by someone who, like them, was also wearing the concentration camp uniform. But very unlike them, he sported an armband that indicated he had been a kapo in a concentration camp. He now appeared quite eager to help the two pathetic figures. He somehow managed to procure a stretcher and recruited some volunteers to assist him in carrying Leibish and Mr. Springer upstairs to the dining room. When they found themselves seated at a table, much like normal human beings would be, they were dumbfounded. After so many months of being treated worse than animals, this felt like royalty! They looked on in astonishment as the former kapo scurried about the elegant hotel like a waiter, bringing them bread, coffee, and other delectables. As Leibish and Mr. Springer pounced on the food ravenously, their waiter cautioned them to refrain from overdoing it since their stomachs would not be able to tolerate the sudden influx of too much food after so many months of starvation.

After eating their fill, Leibish and Mr. Springer would have liked nothing better than to rest their weary bones in a proper bed. However, they were informed that would not be possible in these facilities. This hotel could provide them only with food, after which they would have to leave the premises. No lodgings were available.

Mr. Springer and Leibish were intrigued. Who was sponsoring these meals, and what was this kapo turned waiter doing here? How did he get here? As it turned out, they didn't have to wait long for their curiosity to be satisfied. The kapo/waiter came by their table and seemed quite amenable to share his story.

As an inmate in the Dachau concentration camp, he was, due to certain circumstances, led to the ignoble role of kapo. At some point he was dispatched to this hotel, which housed a Nazi seminary, to work as an attendant/janitor for the faculty and students. Later, as the war drew to an end and Nazi defeat was imminent, both faculty and students dispersed. The kapo then asked the hotel management to be allowed to stay on as a waiter. He suggested to them that, in view of the fact that the Americans were almost upon them, it might serve them well to make their premises available to camp survivors and serve them free nourishing meals. In this way they would curry favor with the Americans and hopefully counter their offensive accommodation of a Nazi seminary.

Finally, the former kapo came to the point: the reason he was recounting all this was that he had a request to make of Mr. Springer. Since there was a possibility that the Americans would make him stand trial for his role as a kapo, Mr. Springer's testimony on his behalf could be invaluable. He implored Mr. Springer to emphasize the compassion and kindness he had observed the man display toward the former Jewish inmates. The fact that he had interceded with the hotel management so that the former inmates would receive free meals was also worth recalling. Mr. Springer was the oldest inmate the kapo had ever come across. Hence, his testimony could be expected to carry more weight than that of any youngster.

Seeing how badly the former kapo was in need of his goodwill, Mr. Springer attempted to cajole the former kapo into somehow obtaining permission for himself and Leibish to be allowed to lie down in a proper bed for a bit. But the kapo/waiter insisted that the hotel was still under German ownership as indicated by the presence of the armed German guard near the doorway. Although he had obtained permission for the refugees to receive free meals, there was no way they would be allowed to utilize any beds there.

The abject pair was left with no other option but to once again set out in search of a place to rest their weary bones. Realizing that the city was still very much under German jurisdiction, they felt impelled to get away from Mittenwald as fast as they could. They decided to make for the local train station. But when they got there, they found it in ruins. There were no trains and no functional tracks. Their attempts to rest there were quickly thwarted by a guard who would not even let them approach the information booth. He did, however, share one piece of information with them: there were no trains. If they wanted to go from one city to another, there was only one mode of transportation available—walking.

And that is precisely what they did. They began traipsing out of Mittenwald, hoping to find some sort of roof over their heads and hopefully, finally, some sort of bed before the sun set. Suddenly, they heard an explosion of gunshots, which was followed by a surge of people—both soldiers and civilians—fleeing in the opposite direction, toward Mittenwald. In their panicked flight, the people did not give the two wandering Jews a second glance. Unhindered, Leibish and Mr. Springer continued their trek away from Mittenwald.

Eventually, they came to a bridge where an armed sentry stood. Meekly, they approached him and asked if they might cross the bridge. He looked the ragged pair up and down before explaining to them that this bridge led directly to the front where war was still raging. "I really don't think it's a good idea for you to go there," he advised. Mr. Springer proceeded to tell the guard a little about what they had been through, how the hotel in Mittenwald had turned them away, and how they literally had nowhere to lay their heads down. The sentinel shrugged and waved them on. As an afterthought, he mentioned that the bridge was heavily mined and gave them some tips how to avoid road mines.

Later they realized how fortunate they were that Mr. Springer, in his fluent German, had managed to get on the guard's good side, enabling them to cross. Other refugees whom they later met related how hostile and unyielding the guards had been with them and how they refused to let them cross the bridge.

The sun was already setting, and the weary travelers had still not found any lodging. By now the sounds of gunshots had abated, and they met hordes of retreating German soldiers fleeing in the direction from where they had just come—a clear indication that the Americans had captured the area.

A desperate situation calls for desperate measures. Hence, Leibish and Mr. Springer were once again reduced to knocking on the doors of local houses, begging for a place to sleep. But, as happened during all their previous efforts, no one was forthcoming. Each of the residents had a different reason why they couldn't accommodate them. Some were ostensibly still afraid of the Germans and did not want to be caught harboring Jews. Others did not even bother giving any excuses.

Before long a heavy rain mixed with sleet started falling. The two wanderers were forced to trek through barren fields. Eventually they reached a little shanty on top of a hillock. The door was locked, and there was no answer when they knocked. Peering through a window, they saw that there was no one there, and they desperately forced their way in. What met their eyes was nothing short of a veritable paradise. There was a little kitchen there, replete with an oven that still had some glowing embers. There was also a pile of firewood there and, miracle of miracles, some carrots and potatoes as well! Last but not least, there was a small bedroom there with several beds.

Leibish and Mr. Springer surmised that the hut must belong to some shepherds who worked all day tending their sheep which grazed in the surrounding fields and mountains and used the hut to rest at night.

Leibish and Mr. Springer added some firewood to the oven and basked in its warmth. Glancing out the window, they spotted two Jews—apparently former concentration camp inmates trudging by like them—who were clad in rags and thoroughly soaked from the rain. Leibish and Mr. Springer hurried to invite them in so that they might share their repast of potatoes and carrots as well as the warmth from the fireplace. The two "guests" were more than delighted to accept the invitation. No sooner had they entered when the four Jews recognized each other as former camp mates from the abysmal Dachau concentration camp. The meal was quite poignant—the tears they all shed were more abundant than the food they shared.

Leibish Makes a Promise

Suddenly, the deafening roar of bombs reverberated through the air. Bombs were falling so close that it seemed like the entire hut was on the verge of collapsing. Still, the four refugees considered themselves fortunate to be inside the flimsy protection of the hut, rather than anywhere outside.

However, their "good fortune" lasted about two hours, after which they were very rudely jolted out of their mini paradise. Without any warning, a burly man with a sullen expression stormed into the hut. "What are you doing here?" he demanded indignantly, looking around at the pathetic group. Before they could stammer a reply, he curtly informed them that he and several other local laborers, who would be returning very shortly, resided in that abode. He minced no words, making it abundantly clear that Leibish, Mr. Springer, and their ilk were not welcome there. He stopped short as his gaze fell on what had once been a respectable pot of potatoes and carrots. He made no effort to conceal his displeasure. "Clearly, you can't compensate us for eating up our food. But you absolutely must leave these premises immediately!" Leibish and Mr. Springer tried reasoning and begging for permission to stay, if only in the kitchen on the floor while he and his friends slept in the bedroom, but to no avail. The uncouth peasant remained deaf to their entreaties, and without any compunction, he turned the pitiable group out to contend with a heavy downpour of rain as well as a hail of bombs and bullets.

For Leibish these were arguably the most frightening moments of the entire war. Throughout all the months of torture and suffering, it was painfully clear to all of them that each moment might be their last. Indeed, each and every one of the camp survivors had looked death in the eye many times over in the course of their interment. But now, having come this far, where Nazi whips and rifles were no longer being brandished over his head, with liberation so imminent, Leibish could not bear the thought of dying from a stray bullet.

In those terrifying moments, Leibish closed his eyes and made a solemn promise: if Hashem delivered him from this peril and allowed him to live, he would make sure to complete a *masechte* every year. And, true to his word, Leibish did indeed make a *siyum* on *masechte* Pesachim every year. This was in addition to the *siyum* on a different *masechte* which he made every year on Erev Pesach.

Trudging past a bombed-out grocery store, they noticed a case of synthetic honey. Desperately hungry as they were, the roving Jews pried the lids open and ate some of it before continuing on their way. Finally, they came to a shack that was filled with hay. The four bone-weary wayfarers burrowed into the hay and fell asleep almost instantly from sheer exhaustion.

Dawn found our wanderers up and about. When they discovered an oven and some pots, they put some snow inside a pot and put it up to boil. And soon there was a warm drink for them to start their day with.

The four Jews realized that they were now free; however, freedom was only a figure of speech, not something that meant anything to them. The date was May 1, and somebody pointed out that it was Lag BaOmer. Hopefully, the *zechus* of the *tannai* Rabbi Shimon Bar Yochai would stand them in good stead, and they would merit seeing personal miracles. With renewed strength and spirits, they continued on their way, not knowing where they were going and unsure of where they ought to go.

CHAPTER 10

Liberated

Finally, under American Jurisdiction

AFTER TWO DAYS OF wandering together, the four refugees felt as if they had known each other forever as they shared their tragic stories and experiences. Suddenly, they heard the roar of tanks in the distance, and before long, they saw a column of tanks lumbering toward them. When they observed the stars and stripes of the American flag on the tanks, their joy knew no bounds. Not having any white cloths to display as a sign of surrender, the four simply sprinted across a field until they were alongside the machines. The soldiers did not need any introductions or explanations. One look at the emaciated figures with the hollow sunken eyes told them all they needed to know. These could only be survivors of the horrendous Nazi death camps. The soldiers were appalled and horrified. They had never seen anyone in such a pathetic state in their entire lives.

The soldiers reached into their knapsacks and withdrew all kinds of food-stuffs (i.e., chocolates, cookies, candies) and began tossing it to the emaciated skeletons standing before them. Someone produced a blanket, which they used to collect the sundry victuals. Ultimately, the small group had more than they could carry.

Right behind the column of tanks there was a convoy of American Army trucks, followed by a car carrying a medical staff. Several soldiers alighted from the trucks and posed for pictures with the survivors. Most of them were literally moved to tears by the sight of the Muselmänner. It was the first time in an awfully long time that the tormented Jews had come across any compassion or sympathy. Only now did they realize that they were truly liberated!

However, there was still confusion and uncertainty. Where should they turn to? Where could they go? Where and how could they begin life anew? The soldiers, too, seemed unsure of what to tell the refugees. One soldier addressed them in broken German and tried giving them directions for how to get to a makeshift kitchen that the American military had set up. He cautioned them to go slowly so that they wouldn't exhaust themselves. Another soldier dismounted his truck and expressed his regret that he couldn't personally guide them. He explained that he was obliged to continue on with his regiment, but if they would wait where they were, he would send a truck to bring them to an American base.

The four weary wanderers were inclined to heed the advice of the second soldier since they were too tired to continue wandering. They decided that, in the meantime, they would eat some of the chocolates of which they now had an overabundance. They reasoned that since they were already suffering from upset stomach and diarrhea, they had nothing to lose.

They waited and waited but no truck came from them. They were still tormented by lice, insect, sweat and grime, and they no longer had the patience to wait. Ultimately, they had to make their way to the kitchen on foot. They tried following the directions they had gotten from the first soldier; however, they found it surprising that they seemed to be the only ones on the road. If this was indeed the road leading to an American established kitchen, why weren't they seeing other people on that road, heading in the same direction?

While they were wandering and wondering, they came across a group of American soldiers standing in a field. It turned out that this group brought up the rear of the column of soldiers they had met earlier. Their friendly, compassionate demeanor was in itself heartwarming. The wandering Jews shared their dilemma with them, that the soldiers they met earlier had been somewhat unclear in their directions, and the group was still uncertain of where to go and what to do.

The soldiers were very forthcoming and immediately offered them coffee and food. Then a female soldier explained to them in German that they were part of an advance contingent whose role was to ensure total surrender in the various towns and cities they came to. They did not have any cars or trucks to transport the weary wanderers to a safe and comfortable haven. However, if they were to walk just a bit further, they would reach an American base, replete with cars, trucks, and lots of kind, friendly personnel.

And indeed, they soon arrived at the American base, and there they were taken to a barrack where food and lodging was being provided to hundreds of refugees. Everyone received two loaves of bread and was welcome to help themselves to onions from huge crates that had been set out there. Then there was a storage chamber filled with sundry articles of clothing where the refugees were encouraged to choose whatever they wanted. And although our wandering group was weak and exhausted and longed to finally lie down to sleep as free men, they realized that perhaps it was better to rid themselves of their lice infested filthy rags and don some clean clothing. They then returned to the barrack where they finally sank into makeshift beds for some much longed-for rest.

After weeks of sleeplessness and exhausting, pointless marches, after so many months of slave labor and unspeakable torture, this was their first peaceful, tranquil night of sleep. By morning many more refugees had joined them in the barrack.

Day of Salvation

An American soldier with an interpreter at his side spoke to the refugees, saying that this was only a temporary arrangement, and eventually the Jews would be provided with more comfortable and permanent accommodations. He explained that as long as the roads were still teeming with soldiers—both American and German—it was unsafe for civilians to be on the roads. Hopefully, the entire region would soon be under American control, and then the Jews would be transferred to an established refugee camp where they could recuperate from their horrific experiences. In the meantime, it would be advisable for them to remain there and rest up from their wandering. The refugees were quite content there and did not at all mind waiting for the eventual transfer to a refugee camp with more resources.

Mr. Springer was still suffering from pain and partial paralysis in his right arm. He asked Leibish to make a fire outside the barrack and prepare something hot to eat or drink. Disregarding his own weariness, Leibish hastened to fulfill Mr. Springer's request. He went outside and scavenged around for some pots and hauled water from a distance. His efforts culminated in the concoction of a sublime hot drink—coffee with sugar!

The parched Jews then indulged in a royal repast of delicious coffee complemented by the chocolate goodies the American soldiers had given them. Slowly, they began to feel better, and their gaunt, emaciated expressions relaxed somewhat. There were even some traces of smiles on the pinched faces.

After breakfast Leibish ambled over to the clothing storeroom and rummaged around. He was delighted to discover brand-new spiffy uniforms. He took one for himself and one for Mr. Springer. Although the uniforms were not the right size for either of them, they were very excited to put them on anyway, hoping to leave the lice on the now-discarded clothing. Mr. Springer looked at Leibish's gaunt, scrawny figure now clad in the new respectable uniform and smiled bitterly. "Do I look as bad as you do?" he quipped.

Lunch consisted of meat and *shlishkes*. This was the first nourishing meal the Jews had had in a very long time. For Leibish and many others, it was more than a year and for others it was as long as six years! Small wonder, then, that all they could think about was food.

Over the next two days Leibish ate shlishkes (which was called macaroni there) again and again. In fact, Leibish subsequently claimed shlishkes as his favorite food since it was the first decent food he ate after the war. He was never really one to make a big deal of his likes and dislikes when it came to food, and his preference for this particular dish was more symbolic of the freedom and liberation that he fortunately lived to see.

Another night passed, and on Thursday morning, May 3, Mr. Springer remarked to Leibish, "You know, I don't think it's worth our while to remain here." He recalled that after WWI there were Red Cross representatives in every train station, administering medical care. He had been hoping to be taken to a medical facility for treatment and delousing. Also, his right arm bothered him immensely, and there was nary a doctor in sight. Moreover, he pointed out, there wasn't even proper administration of the facility they were currently in, and the refugees were pretty much left to fend for themselves. Even the meat and shlishkes that Leibish so relished were not individually doled out to the refugees. Rather, they were set out in a large pot with the hungry men jostling and pushing in order to get their portions.

Although Leibish was unsure and hesitant, Mr. Springer persuaded him to accompany him to Garmisch, a German city where there was supposed to be an established, well-organized American presence. On the way they came across a stash of valuable provisions, which retreating German troops had apparently abandoned in their haste to flee approaching American militia.

Arriving at Garmisch, they knocked on the door of the first house they saw. Predictably, at first, the owners were less than forthcoming. However, after they had a glimpse of the ample provisions that Leibish and Mr. Springer bore, their attitudes underwent a significant change. Leibish and Mr. Springer were invited in, and as the two guests generously shared their bounty with the now cordial hosts, much goodwill was garnered. Ultimately, the hosts assisted Leibish and Mr. Springer in making contact with the American base there. Before long a jeep pulled up, and an American soldier leaped out and invited Leibish and Mr. Springer to board the truck. Then they were transported to an American-run camp. This was on 20 Iyar, May 3, the date that Leibish commemorated as his personal liberation day for the rest of his life, for it was only when he was under total American auspices that he felt completely liberated.

Disappointment in Garmisch

Garmisch-Partenkirchen, in south Germany, is about half an hour's distance from Mittenwald. The Americans retrofitted a hunting lodge there into a refugee camp. But as far as Mr. Springer was concerned, it left a lot to be desired.

Apparently, all their goodwill and compassion notwithstanding, the Americans simply did not comprehend the magnitude of what these refugees had gone through. They weren't just refugees whose dwellings had been destroyed in the war and were now merely in need of housing. These were desperately sick people, wounded and shattered both physically and emotionally, who had suffered endless starvation, torture and trauma, months and years in forced labor and death camps, and unspeakable horrors that only those who were there could fathom. They were in a very precarious state and needed special care and attention, medical and otherwise. This was simply not available in Garmisch.

They had the privilege of choosing a private room, but ironically, it did not include beds or bedding. There was no staff available to support and assist the shattered skeletons of human beings, and they were largely left to fend for themselves. There was a large community kitchen, but there was a serious dearth of food and provisions, and it functioned on a first-come, first-served basis. The very environment was one of disorganization and chaos.

Now that they were technically free, the former death camp inmates began taking stock of what had transpired and wondered about their families and loved ones. Did they still have any? Were any of them still alive? What did the future hold for them? Would they remain in Europe? What about Yiddishkeit? What was left of Klal Yisrael? Would they ever recover from the horrific trauma they had experienced?

As mentioned, they were "technically" free; however, they were still in a camp, surrounded by guards. They weren't free to come and go at will, albeit for their own safety since the war was not yet entirely over, and there were still pockets of combat in the area. In a nutshell, they were still being held in a camp, and they had to find their own bedding and even had to hustle to obtain food.

Tragically, many hapless souls survived the atrocities of war only to succumb in the American-controlled Garmisch.

Mr. Springer's right arm was still paralyzed, but there was no one available to minister to him. Actually, there were some doctors in the camp, but they were of no use to the refugees since they were themselves former inmates of the Nazi camps and did not possess any medical equipment.

Once when the pain was really getting to him, Mr. Springer approached one of the doctors and begged him for help, but of course the doctor could do nothing for him. However, everything is preordained, and eventually, the amount of suffering destined for him was complete.

One day Mr. Springer met a former camp mate—someone who had been together with him in Auschwitz who happened to be a doctor. The man recognized the numbers on Mr. Springer's arm before he recognized his face. Predictably, a friendly conversation ensued, with both of them sharing their tragic post-Auschwitz experiences until their arrival at Garmisch. In the course of their conversation, Mr. Springer complained to the doctor about the pain and paralysis in his right arm. Apparently, this doctor was somewhat more resourceful than the others on the premises, or maybe he just took Mr. Springer's misery more to heart. Or maybe it was a combination of both. He uttered some words that were music to Mr. Springer's ears. "I think I can help you," the doctor declared. "I can give you an injection that will alleviate both your pain and paralysis." The good doctor did not have the medicine with him but posited that it consisted of simple ingredients that were easily obtainable in the camp.

And, true to his word, by the end of the next day, the doctor had concocted a potion that he administered to Mr. Springer. He gave him six more over the next six days. Mr. Springer was grateful and elated as he experienced relief and improvement with each treatment.

A Bold Action—Atoh B'chartonu in the Refugee Camp

Now that he had somewhat recuperated, Mr. Springer's vivacious pluckiness returned. He began plotting and strategizing about how to deal with the lack of food there. Obviously, he couldn't rectify the situation for the entire camp per se, but at least he could for himself, Leibish, and his close circle of friends there. He devised a plan in which Leibish would sneak out of the camp and go into the city to purchase bread. He helped Leibish scale the fence when the guard was distracted, and Leibish landed safely on the other side.

Leibish headed straight to the bakery in Garmisch. Much to his consternation, he found a long, winding line of people waiting to make a purchase—which is not unusual during war time. As Leibish took his place in line, some people recognized him as a concentration camp survivor, thanks to the telltale signs (i.e., his gaunt skeletal frame, sunken eyes, etc.). They immediately let him go ahead of them in the line, otherwise there most likely would not have been any bread left by the time it was his turn.

In the bakery he was allowed to take whatever he wanted and as much as he could carry. Leibish duly filled his pockets with bread and cheese. As he was heading back to the camp with his treasures, he was suddenly stunned to hear the moving lyrics of Yom Tov *zemiros*. Following the singing, he came upon a group of religious Jews who were celebrating the first Shavuous as free men. Leibish eagerly joined them as they davened together and ate the Yom Tov *seudas* together.

As is customary during Yom Tov *seudas,* they sang *zemiros,* including the verse from the Yom Tov *tefillah,* Atoh B'chartonu. In their current situation, these words had a special poignancy, attesting to the eternity of the Jewish nation. After all the trials and tribulations, all the anguish they had suffered—more than any other people in the history of mankind—they were praising Hashem for choosing them from among all other nations of the world and for giving them the Torah.

Leibish never forgot that *seuda* and its accompanying moving lyrics, and for every Yom Tov thereafter, Leibish sang *Ataoh B'chartonu* to the tune that it was sung at that first postwar Shavuous *seuda.*

In this newly formed group of religious Jews, Leibish found solace and comfort, while Mr. Springer sought solace in more mundane pursuits.

When he returned to the camp with his treasure trove of bread and cheese, he was hailed as a hero by Mr. Springer and friends, who were delighted beyond words with the scrumptious spread.

In the meantime, they continued to be plagued by the dearth of food. Scaling the fence had been a one-time feat, which Leibish could not repeat. So Mr. Springer, who was feeling much better and had regained function of his right arm, volunteered to work in the communal kitchen. This gave him a free pass to come and go into the kitchen at will—a perk that enabled him to secure enough food for himself, Leibish, and several other Jews.

A Successful Surgery in the Camp

One day Mr. Springer woke up to the discomfiting realization that his right arm was once again swollen and tender. When he showed his arm to his former Auschwitz camp mate, the doctor, he regretfully informed Mr. Springer that the only option at this point was a surgical procedure.

Unsurprisingly, Mr. Springer was filled with dread. How could he undergo surgery in such a primitive environment? He shared his anguish with Leibish, who commiserated with him no less than if Leibish had truly been his own son. In the end, Mr. Springer steeled himself and decided that for the sake of his wife and children, with whom he hoped to be reunited shortly, he would do whatever it took to regain his health and full function of his arm.

Incredibly, in those primitive circumstances, lacking the most rudimentary medical amenities, the doctor performed the painful but crucial operation, sans the benefit of anesthesia and/or pain medication. As expected, the pain was excruciating, and it took Mr. Springer five weeks to recover.

Throughout the entire ordeal, Leibish never left Mr. Springer's side, waiting on him hand and foot with selflessness and devotion. At the end of five weeks, Mr. Springer was finally fully back to himself. Only then did Leibish begin to indulge in some serious introspection. He and Mr. Springer had grown incredibly close; indeed, they loved each other as only brothers in suffering can. Yet with the passage of time and the healing and recovery that it generated came restiveness and a drive to search for his family. He had no knowledge of what had happened to his loved ones, and he desperately yearned to find out if any of them were still alive. He had heard that there was a transport going to Czechoslovakia, and he was consumed by a desire to join.

With a heavy heart, Leibish revealed to Mr. Springer that he felt he could no longer remain there in limbo, not knowing the fate of his parents and siblings. He felt driven to take this opportunity to return to his hometown in the hope that he might somehow discover his family's whereabouts. And so, amid copious tears and deep sorrow, the two bosom friends took leave of each other with heartfelt promises to keep in touch, but not before Leibish gave Mr. Springer the address of the house in Šaľa where he lived with his parents before the war.

Separated but Ever Connected

Most refugee camps sprouted committees of resourceful survivors who would help their *landsleit* return home. Slowly but surely, the camp in Garmisch emptied out. But Mr. Springer, who hailed from Germany and had nowhere to go, began feeling increasingly uncomfortable and ill at ease there, especially in light of Leibish's departure. He was fed up with being a refugee in a fenced-in camp and pined for independence.

He decided to go job hunting in Garmisch. But unsurprisingly, attitudes among the local German population were still very much in line with those of the just-vanquished Nazis, and no one would give a Jew employment. So Mr. Springer hit on an idea. He modified his modus operandi in his job search and began touting his knowledge of the Polish language, which would surely be an asset to a business. This ability quickly garnered favorable results, and he was hired on the spot. Soon he was able to rent his own apartment.

Now that he was settled, Mr. Springer approached all the organizations and committees that had sprung up at the end of the war to assist survivors locate family members. He submitted his name and those of his wife and children and hoped for the best. After a long and painstaking search, he had the good fortune of finding two of his children—the elder son, Fred, who was already living in the United States and had served in the American Army, and his younger son, Max, who initially lived in London and subsequently joined his older brother in America. Sadly, though, he never found his wife. He remarried and lived in the Five Towns neighborhood in New York until his death in 1985.

Leibish and Mr. Springer kept in touch and remained very close. They rejoiced in each other's *simchos*, and Mr. Springer always made an effort to personally participate in the Gottesman family *simchos*. His signature Bar Mitzvah gift to Leibish's Bar Mitzvah boys was a sterling silver *becher*. In fact, in one instance he gave himself a head start, giving one son, Amrom, his Bar Mitzvah *becher* when he was only eleven years old, lest he not live to see the Bar Mitzvah.

CHAPTER 11

Reunited

Two Brothers—So Close and Yet So Far

As LEIBISH TOOK LEAVE of his friend whom he had grown to love as a brother, he had no inkling that he actually still had a real, bona fide brother in this world.

Remarkably, the two brothers, Kalman and Leibish, both ended up in Mühldorf, a sub-camp of Dachau, with neither of them knowing the other's whereabouts until well after the war was over. Like Leibish, Kalman arrived at Allach, from where he was transported to Mühldorf, where Leibish had been interned since August. However, when Kalman arrived, Leibish had already been sent to the main Dachau concentration camp.

Immediately upon his arrival, Kalman began inquiring about his older brother. When he heard how Leibish had taken ill and was subsequently placed on a truck together with dead and dying people, Kalman came to the distressing realization that his brother was most likely no longer alive.

In Mühldorf, Kalman met two *landsleit*, the brothers Mordechai Dovid and Shabse Reisz who hailed from Kamaron, a village near Šaľa. They used to be regular *mispallelim* at the shul in Šaľa since their village didn't have its own *minyan*. Now, in this Gehinnom, Shabse took the young Kalman under his wing and tried to help him to the best of his meager ability. On one occasion, Shabse advised the young lad to try to integrate into the group that had been designated as infirm, in the hope that this would help him evade the grueling labor.

Kalman, shrewd and resourceful as he was, could have, in fact, maneuvered his way into the group of the feeble and infirm. However, the few months of experience with the Nazi mindset taught him only too well that joining the ranks of strong, able-bodied men would give him a much better chance of survival.

Kalman was later wont to recall a popular children's comic book from Hungary/Slovakia, which featured the narrative of two frogs that had fallen into a huge barrel of milk and were struggling mightily to get out. One frog tried repeatedly to swim to the top of the barrel but kept falling back to the bottom until his strength was totally spent, and he died. The second frog began rapidly kicking his legs, thus churning the milk into butter. As a layer of butter formed at the bottom, the frog stood on it and continued his kicking until yet another layer of butter formed. He did this until he reached the top.

Likewise, a person who finds himself in a quandary ought not always follow their natural instincts, but instead think outside the box.

Kalman often mentioned how he credited his mother's frequently proclaimed confidence in his resourcefulness and survival skills for his ultimate survival in the Nazi inferno. His will to live was further heightened by his longing to retrieve his mother's rings.

Later, while they were in Mühldorf, Shabse took ill and reached a point of extreme weakness—so much so that he lost his will to go on. "What's the point of struggling?" he muttered weakly. "I don't have the strength for this endless suffering." He even considered ending his suffering by hurling himself onto the tracks.

But the young Kalman would have none of it. With incredible maturity and presence of mind, combined with genuine devotion, the young lad soothed and comforted the despairing man, reassuring him that their current situation, grim as it was, was not permanent; things would improve, and they would eventually (hopefully sooner rather than later) be returning home to their families and to a world where normalcy prevailed. Besides words, the only means he had at his disposal to bring Shabse some comfort and relief was snow, which he tried rubbing onto his chest to rejuvenate him. Miraculously, Shabse recovered, and both he and Kalman plodded on, comforting and reassuring each other throughout their gruesome trials and tribulations.

Kalman was assigned to backbreaking labor in the Weltz factory, where huge bomb-proof bunkers with eight-foot-high concrete walls were being erected. Conditions there were brutal, and the cold was literally bone-chilling. Kalman felt that he would not survive it and began looking around for ways to circumvent the grueling work; eventually, he came upon a solution.

Kalman noticed that there was a system in place by which people were assigned to a particular work detail: every morning all the kapos of their respective barracks would herd their inmates onto a designated spot where several contractors were lined up. Each of the contractors would request a specific number of workers for a specific work detail. For instance, one contractor might require twenty people for excavation work, while another would need thirty carpenters, and so forth. The kapos would then provide each contractor with whatever number of laborers he requested. Kalman hit upon a plan in which he deliberately planted himself at the end of the line so that the quota of workers was filled before he was next in line.

This plan worked for a few days, but eventually Kalman's kapo caught on that Kalman had been staying behind and not working for several days. When he confronted Kalman about it, Kalman's heart sank. What kind of punishment and/or wicked plot would the kapo devise for him now? Imagine his astonishment when he heard the kapo say, "Come with me to my office. I want you to clean it every morning and replenish the wood in the oven. I want you to make sure the room is always clean and warm when I come home."

Kalman was dumbfounded. What wonderful *hashgacha pratis*! This was nothing short of a miracle. Not only was he not being punished for shirking work, but he was officially absolved from that dreadful work assignment in the brutal cold. He now had a nice, cozy, and relatively easy job to do, and he got to spend the day in a warm, toasty environment. Moreover, another unexpected boon of this job was that, in the process of lighting the fire and stoking the embers, the lice that were crawling all over his body were exterminated from the heat. As he brushed the dead bugs off, he realized that this was the first time in a long time that he had some relief from the pesky insects.

Included in the kapo's responsibilities was fetching the rations of bread from the kitchen and distributing them among his underlings. When Kalman entered the office on the first day and saw the food lying there, he was overcome by hunger and temptation. However, he resisted and did not touch any of it. But he did take the liberty of searching the garbage pail where he was "fortunate" enough to find some scraps of food to somewhat still his gnawing hunger.

Then he got an idea whereby he might obtain a little more food. He approached another kapo and volunteered his services. "If you like, I can clean your office and keep it warm for you as well." When the second kapo agreed, it meant that Kalman now had the "luxury" of foraging in a second garbage can for precious scraps of food. However, Kalman took a grave risk here since this kapo was notorious for his ill temper and malicious disposition. Woe was the unfortunate inmate who did something to displease him (which didn't take much). His methods of punishment were ruthless (i.e., withholding the meager portion of bread, etc.). In fact, Kalman later had the opportunity to get a bird's-eye view of his malevolence as he observed the kapo pilfering some of the bread that he should have been distributing to his charges.

As Kalman and other concentration camp alumni soon learned, there were two kinds of kapos in the camps. One kind performed their unsavory jobs under duress, forced by the SS barbaric slave drivers. Then there was the other kind who seemed to relish the opportunity of tormenting others, which somehow gave them a certain thrill and a feeling of power.

Still, a desperate situation calls for desperate measures, and Kalman's hunger had reached desperate proportions. So in the end, Kalman overcame his hesitancy and asked for the job. Since then, "lucky" Kalman had two rooms to clean and keep warm and two garbage cans where he might find some discarded scraps of food. Apparently, the *zechus* of the Parshas Ha'mon, which he had recited with such fervor together with his brother Yossi, was still benefiting him. Kalman often speculated that this sudden, inexplicable access to the precious food scraps was due to the *zechus* of the *gemilas chessed* that his mother was wont to do, which included having her children bed down on the floor in order to accommodate needy guests.

In the course of his work there, Kalman saw firsthand the depths to which a self-hating Jew could sink. He noticed that this kapo preferred giving the lighter jobs to Hungarian non-Jews rather than to Jews, despite the fact that this job meant easier access to food and a warm environment, both of which were life savers. As much as it pained him, though, Kalman could do nothing about it.

So he continued performing his duties to the best of his abilities and was happy to have the extra food and to spend time in a warm room.

One day the kapo stormed into his office, bellowing at the top of his lungs, "You are a thief!" he yelled. "I'll teach you!" And to Kalman's astonishment, the kapo threw him out of the office, shouting and cursing that he no longer wanted him for the job. Later, during the daily Appell count, the kapo yanked Kalman out of the line and dragged him over to the senior German officer, declaring that Kalman deserved a vigorous beating as well as an assignment for the most strenuous labor available.

The SS commandant was only too happy to comply, and Kalman suffered immensely, as if to make up for the "good times" he enjoyed while working in the kapo's warm office. Ultimately, Kalman's self-preservation instincts kicked in, and he decided to avoid the Appell altogether. There was no way he could withstand the brutal conditions the evil kapo inflicted on him.

Accordingly, Kalman sought out a hiding place in the barrack. In the back, behind the three-tiered wooden bunk beds, there was a laundry room and a lavatory. There was a low attic above the laundry room, underneath the outer roof. Kalman clambered up to that attic and hid out all day.

When it was discovered that Kalman was missing from Appell, the SS used sniffing dogs to track him. But as soon as the dogs came to the laundry room, they lost his scent due to the strong scent of the chemicals in the detergents. In the evening when his barrack mates returned, the first kapo (the one who first gave him the job of cleaning and warming his office) told him, "You are indeed lucky that you hid out today. My colleague (the second kapo) had a very daunting schedule prepared for you."

The next morning found Kalman in a quandary. He couldn't hide out again and avoid Appell. Predictably, the wicked kapo assigned him to a most grueling work detail where he was sure to freeze to death. Kalman made the rash decision to simply refuse to go to work. He sat down on the ground in a corner and remained there until an SS approached him, brandishing his rifle and threatening to shoot him. Kalman tried reasoning with him: "Why would you shoot me? I didn't do anything wrong."

While Kalman was begging for his life, another SS officer suddenly turned up and yanked Kalman away. "Let me deal with him," he said gruffly. "I know what to do with the likes of him." Apparently, Kalman had a special *Syatto Dishmayo*, because he seemingly found favor in the eyes of this SS officer, which may have very well saved his life. Moreover, this officer was a manager in the kitchen and gave Kalman a job there.

In that environment, a job in the kitchen was equivalent to a ticket to paradise. Kalman was clearly seeing the blessed effects of the aforementioned Parshas Ha'mon, which was once again facilitating his access to food. Notably, though, while Kalman did have access to food, he wasn't exactly having a picnic there. The SS officers and the other non-Jewish kitchen workers were indeed able to eat and drink to their hearts' content. Conversely, Kalman and the other Jewish workers were treated like dogs and were made to retrieve their food from the filthy floor where it was deliberately tossed.

One evening Kalman asked the kitchen manager about the large pots of soup that remained on the stove. The Nazi shrugged. "Oh, that? No one needs that. If you want it, you can have it," he remarked carelessly. Kalman was of course delighted. However, this was just one more indication of the extent of German cruelty. This bland, watery soup was not costly or difficult to produce, and there was obviously plenty of it. To the sickly, starving Jews, this would have been a lifesaver since it was still better than nothing—if only for its warmth. Yet the cruel barbarians could not be bothered to properly distribute the lifesaving liquid to them, preferring instead to let it go to waste since "no one needs that."

For Kalman, the "unneeded" soup became a veritable gold mine. He easily found scores of inmates who eagerly welcomed the tepid liquid that would warm their insides, and they gladly paid for it with some bread. Hence, Kalman now had enough bread as well. The power of Parshas Ha'mon!

In the course of his work in the kitchen, Kalman frequently saw the second kapo that he had worked for come into the kitchen to pick up the bread for the inmates in his charge. Kalman well remembered how this venomous, self-hating Jew had tried his best to get Kalman killed and therefore tried to keep his distance from the kapo. Still, he couldn't help noticing the despicable man's disgraceful overtures to a Hungarian gentile woman who worked in the kitchen. And he suddenly understood why this coward went out of his way to give Hungarian non-Jews the easier, comfier jobs, rather than his own brethren—it was to curry favor with this Hungarian woman.

Like in Auschwitz, the SS doctors were to check the inmates for scarlet fever. When someone in Kalman's barrack was found to have the dreaded disease, the whole barrack was quarantined. Kalman was adamant in his conviction that he had to avoid being part of the group of sick people. As soon as the quarantine was announced he sidled out of that barrack. Once again it seemed that his guardian angels were watching over him. This move literally saved his life because within a matter of hours, that barrack was quickly "liquidated."

Kalman on the Death March, Finally Liberated

When rumors began circulating in Mühldorf about the approach of the Allied Forces, Kalman decided that enough was enough; he was through with working for the glorious Third Reich. He began scheming about how to get himself into the camp hospital where he would hopefully be washed and be allowed to sleep in a proper bed.

His reasoning was that if the need to flee arose, either because of the arrival of the American forces who would liberate them or because the Nazis would make them flee ahead of the arrival of the Allied Forces, he would be able to flee from the hospital. And if they were to remain there for a while, he would at least be able to rest up in the hospital for several days. Kalman was a very determined young man, and when he decided on a course of action, he was usually resourceful enough to make it happen. He presented himself at the hospital, ostensibly with a high fever, and was duly admitted. Of course, the admitting staff had no way of knowing that Kalman had doctored the thermometer to generate a bogus high temperature reading.

No sooner had Kalman settled himself into the hospital when pandemonium broke out. The usually imperturbable Nazis were scurrying around like poisoned mice. They were clearly in a panic. According to rumors, the American soldiers were already almost upon them. Frantically, the SS issued the command, "Schnell! *Raus*!" Obviously, all the Nazi officers and their obliging minions sought to flee before the advancing American soldiers arrived, in order to escape the justice and retribution they so richly deserved. Yet even on the verge of their own downfall, their deep-rooted hatred of the Jews was still seething in their wicked hearts: rather than just fleeing the camp to try to save their own lives, they were still focused on the wretched, barely alive Jews. They could not bring themselves to leave the living skeletons there for the Americans to offer sustenance and succor to. Instead, they ordered the half-dead Jews to line up for a brutal march to the main camp, Dachau, which was quite a distance from Mühldorf.

True to form, the Nazis settled themselves into a bus where they could ride in comfort, while the emaciated prisoners were expected to trudge along on foot. When they had to traverse a steep incline, the bus stalled. But the ever-resourceful Nazis had the ideal solution. Disembarking from the bus, they demanded that their prisoners push the bus up the slope. The quick-witted Kalman made a snap decision. No way was he going to expend what was left of his energy, pushing a bus uphill on behalf of the Nazis. Instead, he sidled onto the bus, curling into a ball underneath a seat, and stayed there until they reached Dachau.

In a remarkable happenstance, unbeknownst to Kalman, there in Dachau he was but two barracks away from his brother Leibish. Soon after their arrival, the Jews were rounded up for one of the infamous death marches to the west of Germany. This death march, as its name implies, notoriously killed scores of weakened Jews who had survived the brutal death camps.

Since the main roads were cordoned off, the poor Jews were made to traipse over long stretches of fields and forests. In the meantime, the mounting reports of American forces drawing increasingly closer served only to intensify the Nazis' resolve to keep the Jews marching along to prevent their inevitable liberation by the Americans.

Eventually, Kalman reached a point where he felt that he had nary an ounce of strength left. In a whisper, he confided to the Jews trudging listlessly alongside him, "I'm going to duck onto the side of the road and hide out. I cannot continue this brutal march anymore."

This was a calculated risk that Kalman was taking. Typically, anyone who dared step out of the column or who lagged behind was summarily shot. However, the Jews were aware, as were the Nazis, that liberation was in the air, and the Americans were too close for comfort. And maybe, just maybe, that would give the Nazi barbarians some pause. Abruptly, the Jew near him whispered to Kalman, "If you make a run for it, then so will I." Before long another followed suit, then another, until there were half a dozen exhausted men who managed to reach into the recesses of their very being and muster the strength which they didn't even know they had. With one swift leap they fell pell-mell on top of each other by the side of the road, waiting with bated breath for Nazi bullets, which, wonder of wonders, did not come! Apparently, the Nazis realized that the brutal power they had so ruthlessly wielded over their hapless captives was no more. The Jews watched incredulously as the long column of weary prisoners trudged past them. When they finally dared look around, they found themselves alone in an unknown location in Germany.

Kalman was still wary of Nazi bullets, albeit from a distance. Huddling with his five companions, he determined that three of them were fluent in the German language—a notable boon as long as they were on German territory. He then paired each of those three up with one of those who did not speak German, instructing them to disperse, each pair fleeing in a different direction so that any German bullets trained at one of them would not hurt another. Thankfully, though, no bullets were forthcoming.

Kalman and his companion began walking, unsure of which direction to go. Seeing a house in the distance, they directed their steps there. When they reached the house, they initially held back, fearful of what might await them behind that closed door. Eventually, however, they had no other choice and knocked timidly. Thankfully, their trepidation was for naught; the occupants of the house received them cordially and gave them food. Listening to the radio there, they learned that the American forces were twenty kilometers away. Their hosts even suggested that they were welcome to stay there and wait out the war's end.

Not surprisingly, Kalman and his companion were somewhat disinclined to put much trust in German hospitality, and they chose not to remain in the house for long. They trudged along aimlessly, unsure of where they were and where to turn. They eventually came across a group that was composed of both Greeks and Jews. After a stretch, their leader ordered them to separate, with the Jews forming one group and the Greeks another. Intuitively, Kalman realized that it would be safer for him to blend into the group of Greeks. However, when the group entered a Greek Orthodox church, he held back. How could he be sure that he wouldn't be shot within the walls of that massive structure? Hiding out behind the building certainly seemed a safer option. So he bedded down in the church yard for the night. Waking up in the morning, he found himself face to face with the glorious vision of an American soldier. While he was still rubbing his eyes to make sure he wasn't hallucinating, the American waved to him and pronounced the magic words, "Hi, you are liberated; you are free!"

The soldier brought Kalman over to his regiment, where he was very warmly received and offered some food. Quickly picking up on the kindliness and compassion of the Americans, he set his aspirations on more than merely food. "Perhaps someone here would be kind enough to take me back to my hometown?" One of the soldiers promptly responded. "Sure, no problem, young man. Just stick with us as we travel through the villages and cities until we arrive at your hometown. You'll be much safer this way."

Kalman related that his experience with the local populace of the various cities, both in Germany and in Czechoslovakia, was quite positive. Invariably, he was received quite kindly and even offered food. One exception was the city of Bratislava (Pressburg). There he encountered only unfriendliness and even downright hostility. It was as if the Bratislavians could not come to terms with the disappointing fact that, against all odds, some Jews did survive Hitler's atrocities and were actually returning home.

Mesiras Nefesh for Morality

In that immediate postwar period, chaos and mayhem reigned supreme. In the time it took for law and order to be restored to the respective countries and provinces—criminality and immorality were the order of the day. Especially vulnerable were young women and girls. Armed Russian troops, who had helped secure Allied victory on the eastern front, roamed the streets restively. Accountable to no one, they preyed with impunity on the defenseless young women.

As Leibish was on the train traveling home to Czechoslovakia, he observed with disgust the unrestrained immoral decadence of the Russian soldiers. In one instance, a gang of armed Russian thugs boarded the train during a station stop and scrutinized the crowd lewdly. Realizing their intentions, Leibish courageously pulled himself up to his full height and deliberately blocked the small group of young Jewish girls who happened to be on the train from the view of the vulgar Russians, effectively shielding them from the evil designs of the depraved men.

Two Sole Remnants of the Family Find Each Other

As the train drew ever closer to Šaľa, Leibish was overcome with longing for his parents and siblings. Imagine his crushing disappointment when he finally reached his hometown and found no vestige of family or anything the family ever owned. He recalled how his mother had instructed that her rings be concealed behind the house. But much to his chagrin, he found no trace of them either—no memento or souvenir of his parents whatsoever.

Sad and disappointed, Leibish remained in Šaľa for a while, wandering aimlessly around the city. He knew there was no future for him there and no reason for him to stay. Yet he stayed on—if only because he could think of nowhere else to go. Surely, it was a higher power that was orchestrating Leibish's disinclination to leave his hometown just yet; a few days after Leibish's arrival to Šaľa, he had the surprise of his life—the likes of which was unparalleled by anything he ever experienced before or after. Namely, his brother Kalman suddenly showed up in town alive and (relatively) well!

If Leibish was stunned and delighted beyond words to discover that his brother had survived the horrors of the death camps, Kalman's joy and astonishment way exceeded his brother's since he had spent the previous few weeks mourning his brother's tragic death. They both wept with happiness and relief and couldn't stop thanking Hashem for his *nissim* and *chassadim* that two of their parent's children had survived and would continue the Gottesman legacy.

As happy as he was to see his brother, Kalman was taken aback by Leibish's extremely emaciated figure. At six foot three, Leibish weighed forty-five pounds. Even after the war was over, Leibish did not pounce on food the way most other camp survivors did. At that time, the American Jewish Joint Distribution Committee (JDC) frequently sent food packages to the refugee camps where the survivors were housed. These packages were ravenously snatched up and devoured. Leibish, however, was too refined to snatch and grab food. He was happy with the small jar of coffee granules that ended up in his possession. He had access to water, but not hot water. So he waited for the arrival of a train and then approached the locomotive, which emitted clouds of hot steam that he utilized to heat the water and presto! He had "delicious" black coffee.

Seeing Leibish so gaunt and undernourished made Kalman realize how fortunate he had been that somehow, in the midst of all the horrors that he suffered, he had been blessed with some access to food. Ever since that fateful day in Auschwitz, he mused, when he recited Parshas Ha'Mon so fervently, he had experienced divine providence every step of his excruciating journey.

Kalman always maintained that Hashem helped him only in the *zechus* of his parents' incredible *hachnasas orchim.* Their home was always open to guests of all types and personalities, and his mother always served them as if they were royalty. The children were likewise taught to be respectful and considerate to their guests, regardless of their oddities and idiosyncrasies.

Kalman, who had actually been the one to conceal their mother's rings, knew precisely where and how to look for them. And suddenly, lo and behold, the rings were in his hands. The two brothers were elated to have a tangible memento of their dear mother, a relic of a sweet, happy youth with beloved parents and cherished siblings, which had all gone up in flames.

It is impossible for us in today's world to imagine the desperate privation and poverty that prevailed among the survivors as they struggled to make ends meet and obtain an immigration visa. During that time, in a moment of excruciating need when they were distressfully strapped for cash, the brothers did something which they deeply regretted for the rest of their lives. As incredible as it seems today, from our vantage point of having an abundance of whatever we need (and even plenty of what we merely desire), Kalman and Leibish sold their mother's rings. Yes, the very same rings that they toiled so tirelessly to find, the rings their mother confidently pronounced they would retrieve after the war. It was a decision they made in a moment of weakness and one which hounded them the rest of their lives.

The two brothers then embarked on a daunting mission. They were determined to trace the whereabouts of their father and/or hopefully find out what happened to him. As mentioned, they knew that before the war broke out he had been taken to the notorious Munka Tabor (a division of the Hungarian military), and they had not heard from him since Pesach 1944. Kalman and

Leibish pursued various leads, but the only thing they managed to ascertain was that he had arrived at the Mauthausen concentration camp in Germany where he tragically perished. That was all they were able to discover.

Many years later, Leibish visited the Yad Vashem Holocaust museum in *Eretz Yisrael* and tried to unearth some information about his father, but to no avail.

As per the directive of *rabbanim*, Leibish and Kalman established 10 Nissan as their father's *yahrtzeit,* which coincided with the time that he had been taken away from Šaľa. The 10th day of Nissan also is the *yahrtzeit* of other *tzaddikim*, as well as the *yahrtzeit* of Miriam *Ha'nevueh.*

From that point on, Kalman and Leibish, the two sole survivors of the Gottesman family, were inseparable. Even though their life paths were not identical, the two brothers remained bound by a profound love and deep friendship. While Leibish spent all his days in the study of Torah, Kalman combined his Torah learning with the pursuit of *parnassa.* Yet the mutual respect they had for each other was astounding.

Glossary

a'h: Rest in peace
Atoh B'chartonu: You chose us
B'H: Thank God
Baruch Hashem: Thank God
bechasdei Hashem: By the grace of God
Becher: Kiddush cup
Bitachon: Security
chas v'shalom: God forbid
chassadim: Graces
chinuch: Education
Chizuk: Strengthening
divrei Torah: Discussion of Torah
emuna: Faith
Eretz Yisrael: Land of Israel
gashmius: Worldliness
Gedolei Yisrael: The great men of the Jewish Nation
gemilas chessed: Withdrawal of kindness
groise bashefer: Great creator
gut Shabbos: Good Saturday
Ha'nevueh: The Prophetess
hachnasas orchim: Hospitality
hashgacha pratis: Private supervision
Hatzadik: The righteous
HY'D: God will avenge the blood
IY'H: In God's willing
Isru Chag: day after feast
kabbolas Shabbos: Shabbat prayer
kavanah: Intention

kedoshim: Saints
Kehilla: Community
Klal Yisrael: The Jewish Nation
ketana: Small
lamdanim: Scholars
land verchaft: Field workers
landsleit: Men from same country
limud HaTorah: Torah study
malach: Angel
malach elokim: Angel of God
Malach Hamoves: Angel of Death
Malach Refoel: Angel Raphael
masechte: Tractate
megillah: Scroll of Esther
mekayem: Uphold
mesiras nefesh: Martyrdom
middos: Good qualities
minyan: Quorum
mispallelim: Worshipers
mitzvot: Commandments
nissim: Miracles
oneg: Pleasure
parnassa: Livelihood
Parshas Ha'mon: The Haman affair
pshet'l: Torah argumentation
pshetlech: Torah argumentations
rabbanim: Rabbis
Rav: Rabbi
ruchniyus: Spirituality
segula: Adaptation
selektzia: Selection
seuda: Feast
seudas: Feast
seudas Shabbos: Shabbat feast

shaliach: Messenger

Shalom Aleicham: Peace be upon you!

shechita: Slaughtered

shlita: Shall live long and healthy

shochet: Slaughterer

simcha: Happiness

simchos: Joyous feasts

siyum: Finish

Syatto Dishmayo: Heavenly help

talmid: Pupil

talmid chacham: Torah knowledge

talmidei ha'yeshiva: Yeshiva Talmud

tannai: Sages from the Talmud

Tefillah: Prayer

Tehillim: Psalms

tefillos: Prayers

tish: Occasional feasts

tzaddikim: Righteous

yahrtzeit: Jewish memorial day

yamim tovim: Jewish holidays

ym'sh: Their name will be erased

zechus: Credit

zemiras: Singing

Zoche: Winner

zt'l: A righteous male for blessing

zy'a: His right will protect us

About the Author

AMROM GOTTESMAN WAS BORN and raised with strong values of family, religion, and faith, in part because both of his parents were Holocaust survivors. *Strength from Within* is his father's story.

He was raised in Mount Kisco, New York, and graduated from the Yeshiva of Nitra.

Currently, Gottesman lives in Brooklyn, New York, where he was also born. He is married and blessed with a family of children and grandchildren, and he is an entrepreneur and owner of a successful medium-sized business.

Recently, Gottesman authored an autobiography about his father, R' Leibish Gottesman z'l ("Demis Arya" in Yiddish), a high-demanding, top-selling book.

Printed in Great Britain
by Amazon

26012874R00076